WORKING WITH
FAIRIES

Magick, Spells, Potions, & Recipes to Attract & See Them

ANNA FRANKLIN

New Page Books A division of The Career Press, In
Franklin Lakes, NJ

Copyright © 2006 by Anna Franklin

All rights reserved under the Pan-American and International Copyright Conventions. This book may not be reproduced, in whole or in part, in any form or by any means electronic or mechanical, including photocopying, recording, or by any information storage and retrieval system now known or hereafter invented, without written permission from the publisher, The Career Press.

WORKING WITH FAIRIES

EDITED BY AND TYPESET BY KATE HENCHES

Illustrations by Anna Franklin

Cover illustration and design by Paul Mason

Printed in the U.S.A. by Book-mart Press

To order this title, please call toll-free 1-800-CAREER-1 (NJ and Canada: 201-848-0310) to order using VISA or MasterCard, or for further information on books from Career Press.

The Career Press, Inc., 3 Tice Road, PO Box 687,
Franklin Lakes, NJ 07417
www.careerpress.com
www.newpagebooks.com

Library of Congress Cataloging-in-Publication Data

Franklin, Anna.

Working with fairies : magick, spells, potions & recipes to attract and see them / by Anna Franklin

p. cm.

Includes index.

ISBN 1-56414-824-6 (paper)

1. Fairies. I. Title.

BF1552.F73 2005

133.4'3--dc22

2005053438

DEDICATION

For Ron and Maureen

Contents

3
TECHNIQUES
FOR FAIRY CONTACT
58

4
SPIRITS OF THE YEAR
92

5
DEVAS AND DRYADS
102

Introduction

hroughout history, there have been many people who have known and worked with the spirits that we call fairies. Here in Britain, where I live, both the ancient Celts and Anglo-Saxons believed in such beings, a faith that has had a lasting legacy up until the present day. The Celtic name for fairies is *sidhe*, a word that means a burial mound, hill, or earth barrow, because this is where many fairies live. It is said that when the Celts invaded Ireland, the resident people, the Tuatha Dé Danaan—who had supernatural powers—were forced to retreat into the hollow hills and were only occasionally seen after that, though people left offerings of meat and milk on their mounds. They are very tall and thin, eternally young and beautiful in appearance, and generally dressed in white. The Anglo-Saxon term for similar spirits is elf or *aelf*, a word meaning something along the lines of "white spirit," or "shining spirit." They are tall and beautiful and shine with a kind of inner light. They also live in mounds, and people left offerings, called *elf blots*, of meat and milk on the mounds for them.

Fairies inhabit a kingdom called Fairyland, Elphame, or the Otherworld. This realm is not separate from ours, but overlays it, unseen except in special circumstances. Fairies are occasionally glimpsed in our world, but usually only in the blink of an eye or on the edge of dreams. However, there are places where the two worlds sometimes meet;

natural power spots, bridges between the worlds where people have occasionally slipped from the everyday world into Fairyland, perhaps walking into the mist between two old stones, or stepping accidentally into a fairy ring, only to find themselves in a kingdom where it is always summer, where the orchards bear apples and flowers at the same time, and where death and old age are unknown.

There have always been legends of fairies and they exist in every country of the world. The people of ancient Greece and Rome worshipped the nymphs of meadows, streams, and mountains, and the dryads who lived in trees. Ireland abounds with tales of people who have encountered leprechauns who showed them treasure at the end of rainbows, wailing banshees who heralded the death of relatives, and drunken cluricauns who stole from wine cellars. In England there are old pamphlets describing the mischievous antics of Robin Goodfellow, the merry spirit of the greenwood who cared for its animals and played tricks on hunters, and stories of West Country pixies who led travellers astray, but who helped kindly farmers with their work. There are similar fables from Africa, Hawaii, the Americas, Australia, Europe, Japan, China, and Russia.

A culture that believes in fairies is one fundamentally different from our modern Western materialistic society. It recognizes that a life force suffuses the whole of Nature, an energy that manifests in a range of spirits that fill the meadows, streams, wells, forests, and even the air itself. They guard fields and individual trees, mountains and hearth fires. They may bless or curse humans as they please, and inflict sickness or health on the flocks and herds. Not so very long ago, an association with the fairies was a very real part of people's lives. An excellent relationship with the "The Good Neighbours"—as the fairies were called—was essential for the well-being and prosperity of anyone who depended on the land for his or her livelihood. Fairies were given offerings of milk on the old standing stones, bread and salt in the corners of fields, cream in saucers left on the hearth, and were left part of the harvest. Special stones—called *dobby stones* in the Northern counties—had shallow depressions for making offerings to them and were placed by field gates or the farmhouse door. Spiritual guardians called the Ward gathered at dusk in their sacred places, still known as ward trees, ward hills, and ward stones, to guard villages. The Wild Hunt rode out to collect the souls of the wicked. For the countryman, fairies, elves, and natural magick were part of the everyday experience.

As we humans moved away from our close connection to the earth, we lost our link with the wildfolk. We forgot how to see them, how to contact them, and how to treat them. Stories of them persisted, but they lost their awesome status. We diminished them, in our imaginations, into the cute Tinkerbells of nursery tales. Make no mistake: This is not a book about those fictional creatures that appear in storybooks and cartoons or the tiny, tutu-skirted, gossamer-winged beings of Victorian fables. This is a book about real fairies; potent beings of Earth, Air, Fire, and Water, of plant, stream, rock, and place; creatures of raw nature, representing its power and energies. Some of them are benevolent, but some are downright dangerous.

If we are to relearn the ways of working with fairies, the wildfolk of earth, we must follow the ancient pathways through the forest, where it is sometimes dark, frightening, and perilous, and sometimes bright with dappled light, exhilarating, and echoing with numinous power.

1
The Walker
Between Worlds

O nce, every village had a wise woman or cunning man who dealt with the wildfolk. Such people were common in Britain and Ireland right up until the end of the World War I. Their job was to maintain the balance between the human and fairy world, to mediate with the spirits, to solicit their blessings for good harvests, to repair any damage done to their relationships with humans, to placate the forces of blight, to heal, and to remove curses. They inherited the mantle of the old Druids and the ancient priests and priestesses of the Pagan world, who became the witches and fairy doctors of later ages. Both the ancient Celts and Saxons had gifted individuals who were able to journey, at will, into the world of the spirits. In later times, these people were called witches, a name that comes from the Anglo-Saxon *wicce*, or wise one.

WITCHES AND FAIRIES

Witches and fairies were often thought to have the same powers: Both use magick and both can bless and curse. In fact, the old Romany word for "fairy" is the same as the one for "witch." The Irish believed that a witch was created when a young girl spent seven years in the Otherworld with her fairy lover, coming back somewhat aged, but with knowledge of herbs, philtres, and secret spells. The famous witch Biddy Early insisted that her powers came from the fairies. She used a blue bottle, given to her by the fairies, for healing and prophecy. At her death in 1873 it was thrown into a lake so that no one else could attempt to use it.

The old witches worked their magick in conjunction with wildfolk, and there is plenty of evidence for this in the trial records. The accused often tried to explain that their powers came not from devils, but from the fairies. Elspeth Reoch of Orkney, Scotland, confessed, in 1616, that she had met a fairy man who offered to teach her to understand and see anything she wanted. In 1566, John Walsh of Netherberry in Dorset, England, said that he knew when men were bewitched because the fairies told him. When he wanted to converse with fairies he would go to the hills where there were mounds of earth, and speak to them between the hours of noon and one, or at midnight. In 1587, John Penry of Wales spoke of swarms of soothsayers and enchanters who professed to walk, on Tuesday and Thursday nights, with fairies, bragging of having knowledge of them. Fifty years later, a Caernarvonshire, England, man claimed to speak twice weekly with the fairies, again on Tuesdays and Thursdays.

In the 1600s, in the North of England, a man was taken into court on charges of witchcraft. He claimed to use a powder to heal sicknesses, and offered to lead the gentlemen of the court to the fairy hill where he obtained the medicine. He had discovered the hill when he was destitute and agonizing about how to feed his wife and children. A lovely woman had appeared to him and advised him that if he followed her counsel, he would get a good living from it. She led him to a little hill and knocked on it three times. The hill opened and they went in, coming to a fair hall, where a fairy queen sat in great state, with many people about her. She gave him a box full of white powder and taught him how to use it by giving two or three grains to any who were sick, which would heal them. The Judge asked whether the place within the hill (which he called a hall) was light or dark, and the accused replied it was like twilight. After being asked how he got more powder, he said that when he wanted it, he went to that hill and knocked three times, and said every time, "I am coming, I am coming," whereupon it opened. Going in, he was conducted by the beautiful lady to the queen. The outraged judge said that if he were judged guilty, he would have him whipped all the way to the fairy hall, but because he had cured many with his white powder, they acquitted him. Similar stories of witches gaining their powers from fairies were told over and over again all around Britain.

This association of fairies and witches goes beyond the British Isles and seems to have an almost universal resonance in other parts of the world. For example, in parts of Eastern Europe, witches were called *vilenice*, which implies someone who deals with fairies (*vile*). During an investigation in the late 17th century, a young vilenica confirmed that her powers had been granted to her by a fairy who had shown her the properties of herbs and who could be called upon by virtue of certain herbs picked together with their roots. As in other places, there were tales of children and adults disappearing into the mountains for months or years, and returning with magickal powers granted to them by the fairies. In northern Croatia, the people said that on each Good Friday a vile flies down from the sky to teach women how to heal people and be of benefit to them. The women had to go with their hair unbraided into the green grove, where two had to climb the old trees with the vile, and eat yarn, to better remember what the vile was teaching them; in this way they became vilenice.[1]

The Queen of Elphame

Scottish witch trials in particular were often notable for their accounts of the Fairy Queen, or Queen of Elphame ("Elf Home"). Isobel Gowdie said that she met the Fairy Queen when she went into the hollow hills, and learned all her magick from the fairies whilst there. She spoke of the wildfolk that waited upon her coven as Robert the Jakis, Sanderis the Reed Reever, Thomas the Fairy, and Swain the Roaring Lion, but she was stopped from speaking further by the interrogators, as she often was when she spoke of fairies, as can be seen from the transcripts. The interrogators only wanted to hear of devils and evil deeds.

In 1588 Alison Pearson was condemned for "haunting and repairing with the Good Neighbours and the Queen of Elphame." It seems that the Fairy Queen sent messengers to summon likely witches. In 1670, Jean Weir said that, when she kept a school at Dalkeith, a tall woman came to her house. She had a child upon her back and two at her feet. The woman desired that Jean should employ her to negotiate on her behalf with the Fairy Queen. This was how Jean first became involved in witchcraft. Her brother Major Weir offered himself up and was executed as a witch in Edinburgh, refusing all attempts to convert him. In 1576, Bessie Dunlop stated that, as she lay in childbed, a stout woman came and sat down beside her, comforted her and drank with her. The coven leader told her that it was the Queen of Elphame, his mistress.

The old British witches called their supernatural mistress the Fairy Queen, and it was she who led the Sabbat. Similarly, many Italian witches believed in the historical existence of a woman (or goddess) named Aradia, who brought about a revival of Italian witchcraft, travelling the country and preaching the old Pagan religion of Diana, whom they called Queen of the Fairies. There was a Rumanian Pagan sect known as the Callusari who, during the Middle Ages, worshipped a mythical empress who they sometimes called "Arada" (possibly Aradia), naming her as Queen of the Fairies. The *Callusari* dancers were the followers of the Fairy Queen, and their dances were thought to have originated in the Otherworld. Similar Macedonian dance troops were called *Rusalia* or "Fairies." Like fairies, they were responsible for bringing fertility to the land.

The Italian carnival society of the Cavallino assembled under the banner of Erodiade, a name for the Queen of the Fairies, possibly synonymous with the witch goddess Herodias. The society grew to prominence in the Middle Ages, appearing in processions, pantomimes, and healing sessions, but may have had a very ancient, Pagan origin. Exclusively male, its members dressed in women's clothes and wore make-up. They always gathered in odd numbers, such as seven, nine, or eleven. The Catholic Church persecuted them as Pagans who worshipped the goddess Diana.

Before the advent of Christianity, all the peoples of Europe acknowledged a multitude of spirits that inhabited the Earth; similar beliefs exist or have existed throughout the world. The spirits were as much a part of the land as the animals that lived upon it, the birds that flew above it, and the fish that swam in the sea; and equally essential for its life, well-being, and growth. Shrines to these beings were scattered across the countryside. Special trees were protected by fences and decorated with garlands. People made offerings on stones and at wells and rivers. Every sacred place had a spiritual guardian and a human guardian upon whose land it happened to stand.

However, in the Christian world view, trees, rocks, and stones have no spirit and no consciousness, and those who made offerings to the fairies within were deluded. Aelfric, an 11th century inhabitant of the monastery of Cerne Abbas in England, denounced those who made offerings to "earth-fast" stones, trees, and so on "even as the witches teach." The word he used for witches was Wiccan.[2] Such people were condemned as Heathens and Pagans, words respectively meaning "people of the heath" and "people of the countryside." Missionaries destroyed Pagan temples and groves, and cut down sacred trees in an attempt to banish the spirits that dwelt there. However, it was much harder to banish the fairy faith from the consciousness of the people who dwelled close to the land and encountered its wildfolk on a regular basis. The notions of the country people have survived in folklore and folk practice to the present day in the shape of a belief in fairies.

In Christian doctrine, any spirit that is neither saint nor angel is considered demonic in origin, and fairies are included under this heading. According to one Irish belief, those angels that were cast out of heaven for their pride became fairies. Some fell to earth and dwelled there long before man; others fell into the sea and became water fairies. Others fell into hell where the devil commands them. They dwell under the earth and tempt humans into evil, teaching witches how to make potions, spells, and enchantments. King James I's book *Daemonologie* equated fairies with devils in no uncertain terms and advised people who had them in their homes to get rid of them immediately. Writing in 1701 the Orkney vicar Rev. John Brand said that fairies were evil spirits seen dancing and feasting in wild places. English Puritan writers of the 16th and 17th centuries believed all fairies were devils.

If people worked with fairies, it was considered that they had renounced their Christian faith, something often reiterated in the trial records. In 1670 Jean Weir confessed that she had performed a ritual at the bidding of a fairy so that all her troubles would depart. Afterwards she found that she had wonderful ability with spinning, but this made her afraid, and she stayed indoors for 20 days weeping, because she thought that what she had done in working with a fairy was, in effect, a renunciation of her baptism.

Early Christians denounced the gods and spirits of the old Pagan religions as baneful and identified the old Pagan gods as devils. Nymphs, dryads, satyrs, vegetation spirits, and fairies were condemned by the Church as devils. It is often the practice of a new religion to demonize the gods and spirits of the old, rival religion. Sometimes the feeling was mutual, and in the 19th century, when at sea, fishermen on the Moray Firth would never mention such words as "church" or "minister." Any utterance suggestive of the new faith would be displeasing to the ancient spirits of the ocean, and might bring disaster upon the boat.

Witch Blood

Most people go about their everyday lives unaware of the presence of the Otherworld. The vast majority have forgotten how to see the non-physical realm. As children we may see and speak with fairies, but, as we grow up, we are told that this is just imagination; it is not real. As we get older, we become distracted by the material world: the business of falling in love, raising families, and earning a living. We forget the Otherworld until *something* makes us remember.

According to the old lore, not everyone can see fairies; you have to be born with what the Scottish called "the sight," an ability to see into the spirit world and to read the future. It is a talent possessed by the genuine wise woman, the shaman, the witch.

The worker with fairies is a *Walker between the Worlds*, travelling between this realm and the Otherworld. Such a person is one who dwells a little apart from the everyday world and sees further than its boundaries.

The future witch or shaman may be the lonely child who hovers on the edge of social groups, misunderstood by those around him or her because he or she is different, seeing things, hearing things, aware of things that others are not. This is reflected in fairy tales where it is always the orphan or the outcast who contacts the fairy or witch, and who has the adventures. Some people have souls of clay and cleave only to the material realm; others have souls of fire and seek to fly.

People who see the fairies are often called "fey" themselve—that is, fairylike. It was not unknown for seers to have some fairy blood in their veins. It was rumoured that fairies and humans often mated; preachers even denounced human and fairy liaisons from the pulpit. The offspring of such marriages were always wild and strange, their beautiful eyes, and red hair, and bold, reckless temperaments betraying their fairy blood. They were mystics and possessed second sight, or they became legendary warriors, bards, or musicians. Many famous people are thought to have had one mortal and one Otherworldly parent, including Alexander the Great, the Queen of Sheba, and Merlin. Even Shakespeare was said to have been part fairy.

People with fairy blood are passionate, sensitive, and psychic, and if they find their true path may develop into the artists, poets, seers, shamans, and witches of our world: indeed, the heritage is sometimes called the "witch blood."

However, once incarnate in the flesh, many forget their spiritual purpose: to work in harmony with the Otherworld. Ordinary life may take over, but deep inside them there will always be a feeling of something lost, something lying beyond the five ordinary senses: a deep, unfulfilled longing. It may take a dramatic event to re-awaken the connection to the spirit realm—an illness or a loss: what is often described as the *shamanic crisis*. It may be a gentler awakening, as when the older woman, after her children have grown, turns to spiritual matters, and takes on the mantle of the wise woman. There may be many such people among us now— you may be one—ready to be awakened. Those who never remember, never follow their true path, will always feel themselves to be strangers in an alien world; they usually become depressive, vengeful, and self-destructive.

OTHERWORLD INITIATION

Today, people who see fairies and spirits are often derided as delusional, but, in the past, such people were highly honoured. In the *History of the Danes* (written in 1182–1210), Saxo wrote that one had to be a gifted person to see spirits, and went on to explain that such people had probably experienced prophetic dreams in childhood, or had later undergone a sickness that opened the world of spirits to them, thus describing a classic shamanic initiation.[3]

We have already seen that witches derive their powers from fairy spirits, and this may follow a shamanic initiation, whereby a sickness or other desperate situation opens up the Otherworld of spirits to the witch. In 1588, as she lay sick in bed, Alison Pearson was introduced to the world of fairies by her dead cousin, William Sympson, who appeared to her in fairy form. He came to her as a "green man" and told her he would help her if she would be faithful to him. Then he vanished and reappeared with a group of fairies, who persuaded Pearson to take part in their merrymaking. Sympson also told her how to use herbal remedies. Whenever Pearson spoke about the fairies to others, she was tormented with blows that left insensitive spots on her skin. She was convicted of witchcraft and burned at the stake.

In 1623, Scottish witch Isobel Haldane claimed that as she lay in her bed she was taken forth and carried to a hillside where the hill opened and she entered inside. She stayed for three days with the fairy folk, until she was delivered from Fairyland by a man with a grey beard.

One tale that describes an Otherworld initiation is that of Thomas the Rhymer. He had been playing his lute beneath a hawthorn in the woods when a beautiful fairy, riding a white horse, emerged from the trees to listen. Eventually she dismounted and he couldn't resist trying to kiss her. She warned him that such an act would bind him to her for seven years, but he did not hesitate. They journeyed together through the night to a bright meadow in which there were two paths, one to perdition and one to righteousness, but the Fairy Queen explained that for lovers and bards there was another path, a twisting third way that led to Fairyland. While in the fairy world Thomas was shown a mysterious tree which bore magickal apples. The Queen of Elphame warned him that it bore all the plagues of hell, but it also conveyed the gift of prophecy.

After seven years, Thomas returned home, but his songs were sweeter and more poignant than ever before. He was also able to foretell the future, as in Fairyland he had eaten an apple whose flesh had the power of truth, a parting gift from the Fairy Queen. On his 78th birthday, he was holding a party when he was told that two white deer, a male and a female, were heading through the village to his house. He knew this to be a summons to Fairyland and followed them back there, where he still sings and plays.

The apple is the fruit of Otherworld knowledge. The plagues of hell that accompany it are the suffering and pain the shaman must go through to win the sight. Once this is won, and the apple eaten, he or she will never be the same again, and is forever changed. The third way described by the Fairy Queen is the way of the Walker between the Worlds.

2
The Otherworld

The Otherworld, Fairyland, or Elfhame, is the land of the fairies, which coexists with our own. There are many stories of human beings who have accidentally stumbled into it by entering a fairy ring or a fairy mound, or by discovering a fairy island. In Wales there is a certain piece of turf, which if you step on it, will afford you a glimpse of fairyland, though the turf can never be found twice by the same person. The following is a legend from Wales:

A man who lived at Ystradgynlais went out to look after his cattle and sheep on the mountain, and disappeared. After three weeks, when his wife had given him up for dead, he came home. When his wife demanded to know where he had been for so long, he declared that he had only been gone for three hours. He had been playing on his flute at the Llorfa, near the Van Pool, when he was surrounded by a circle of little men, who sang and danced to his music. They offered him some small cakes to eat, of which he partook, and he had never enjoyed himself so well in his life.

An early chronicler called Giraldus Cambrensis documented the Welsh fairy traditions. One event he related took place near Swansea and concerned Elidorus, a priest who, as a 12-year-old boy, ran away from the preceptor and hid under the hollow bank of a river. There he remained hungry for two days, until two little men appeared and invited him to go with them into a country full of delights and sports. The invitation was speedily accepted. He accompanied his guides into a subterranean land, populated by small, kindly people, and ruled by a king. He dwelt in Fairyland for some time, often leaving it by secret paths to visit the ordinary world, until, on one of these occasions, he went to see his mother and told her of the fairies and how they had many gold ornaments and toys. She asked him to bring her a piece of gold, because she was so poor, and as they had so much of it, they wouldn't miss it. Accordingly, on his return to Fairyland, he stole a golden ball as he was playing with the King's son and ran off with it to his mother. The fairies pursued him, retrieved the ball, and in no uncertain terms, reviled the boy who had abused their hospitality by stealing from them. Though Elidorus spent many long years, with penitence and shame, looking for the underground realm, he could never find it again.

Certain places are better than others for making contact with the Otherworld. Those magickal doorways are usually (though not exclusively) in remote areas: the fairy worlds are linked to sacred Nature, and we need to tune into sacred Nature in order to contact the fairy realm. The wildfolk are becoming harder to find as so little of the natural world is undisturbed. Daily more of their habitat disappears, and they have good reason to hate humankind for it. Thus, they are not kindly disposed to the vast majority of humankind, and the would-be Walker between the Worlds will have to prove himself or herself before any contact can be made.

The Earth is a living body, and like the human body, it has energy centres or *chakras*. The ancients marked these with standing stones, circles, temples, and groves. They were places where humans and spirits met, hallowed by time and custom. Many have been forgotten, and some were never known by humankind. However, the sensitive person may recognize them as places of numinous power by the slight feeling of tension in the air, and by the fact that they are physically unusual in some way. They stand out from the landscape around them, perhaps having unusual rock formations, strangely twisted trees, and so on. When you find such a place, you will *know*.

The places where fairies live are all thresholds of some kind. Boundaries are charged with power; they are magickal places between places—or times between times—belonging to neither one thing nor the other, forming points where the Otherworld can intersect with this one. These boundaries might include such in-between things as crossroads, the shore between sea and land, thunderstorms, midnight (the time between one day and the next), dawn, sunset, New Year's and Halloween (the time between summer and winter).

FEY FOLK DWELLINGS

Doorways

The threshold of a house is an uncertain place, neither inside nor outside, but a boundary between the two. When a person crosses a threshold he or she moves from one state to another and may be in danger from the spirits that dwell *between,* as many spirits do. In many cases, it was thought unlucky to tread on the threshold itself, and people were always careful to step over it. This is why brides, in a transitional stage of life, are carried across it. A number of fairies live beneath thresholds, including the French Follets (who are bad-tempered but will act as house fairies if you win their respect) and the Russian house fairy, the Deduška Domovoy. Because not all fairies are kind or welcome, the Irish scattered primroses on the doorsteps to keep them from crossing it, and in England thresholds were made of protective holly wood for the same reason. In parts of Britain, defensive designs called "step patterns" were drawn on the doorstep in salt or chalk, or reproduced in mosaic. These took the form of knot work and "tangled thread" patterns because the fairies like to follow straight paths when travelling and get caught up in trying to follow the twisting lines.[1]

Hearth

Hearth stones were similarly decorated, because the hearth is a threshold too. There are many fairies associated with human hearths, and they often gain entrance to homes via the chimney or smoke hole. One such is the Italian house fairy the Attilio who, like his Welsh cousin the Bwciod, likes to warm himself by the fire. Both become angered if people try to keep them out by such methods as putting ash on the fire or placing a piece of iron on the hearth. The Italian Fireplace Folletti live in the hearth and many other fairy homes lie beneath hearths, with the hearthstones as their doors. In Italy, at the Feast of the Epiphany, children hang up stockings for the fairy Befana to fill with gifts. She was once a deity of fate. In Germany the hearth is associated with the fairy Perchta, once a goddess of the hearth fire, home, and marriage.

In the past, the hearth was the central focus of the home, providing warmth and food. It was the place of the fire, which meant the difference between freezing and surviving, eating and starving. As such it was sacred and the focus of many customs. The fire had to be kept burning, as it was, or represented, the living spirit of the home, and was only put out at certain times of year, to be re-lit from a sacred flame.

Because the smoke rose to the sky, it was a message rising to the gods, while below the hearthstone lay the underworld. Therefore the hearth was also a domestic *cosmic axis* via which the gods or spirits could enter the home and a shaman's spirit could travel out; this is why Father Christmas enters the house via the chimney.

Gateways

Gates on old roads and paths are magickal boundaries, and often the place where fairies are seen. In Wales, it is said that a fairy sits on every stile. Cunning men often used field gateways as places to perform magickal operations.

Bridges

A bridge is neither on land nor on water, and therefore shares the magick of liminal places; a curse broken on a bridge will be washed away. Bridges are frequented by various types of fairies, such as the lovely White Ladies who ask passersby to dance with them. If the travellers are polite, the fairies will bless them. If they are rude and refuse the request, the fairies will toss them into the river to learn better manners.

On the Isle of Man is the Ballona Bridge ("Fairy Bridge"), which no local will cross without offering his or her greetings to the little folk beneath.

In Sweden, people can visit bridges to meet with the water fairies called the Naecken to ask them to bestow the gift of music. A fiddle is hung beneath the bridge on three consecutive Thursday nights. On the last night, the seeker will find two fiddles hung there, and he must choose his own. If he does, he will become a great and famous musician, but should he choose the Naecken's instrument, the water fairy will take his soul.

Bridges can be dangerous places because they are also the domain of trolls, who lurk beneath them, attacking animals and throwing stones at humans.

Fords

Several fairies were encountered at fords, and there were special shrines for the traveller to invoke the ford spirits to allow him or her to cross the river or to give thanks for being allowed to cross safely.

Wells

Wells represent life force and always contain a spirit. They also act as entrances to the spirit world, where people can go to speak to the gods or fairies, perform divinations, or make offerings. Many wells, when excavated, have been found to contain numerous gifts of pins, pottery, bronzes, and so on.

Water fairies have healing powers, and their help is still solicited in parts of Britain with offerings of coins thrown into wells. A well near Penrhos in Wales allegedly cured cancer. The sufferer would have to wash in the water, curse the disease, and drop pins into the well. Some special trees, called *cloutie trees*, which grow near holy wells and springs are hung with rags (clouties) to solicit blessings or healing from the spirits. As the rag disintegrates, the wish will be fulfilled. (Those people who hang up bits of plastic tape misunderstand the custom, and not only will they be disappointed in their hope, they will also anger the wildfolk by polluting the environment.)

In England, principally in Derbyshire, well-dressing customs are still enacted every year, during which wells are decorated with pictures made of flowers. These were originally constructed to honour the well spirits, though the events now take place under the auspices of the local churches and the themes of the pictures are biblical ones. The wells, which were once shrines of the spirits of healing waters, have been re-dedicated to Christian saints with similar names such as Anne (Anu), Brigit (Brighid), and Helen (Elen). Almost every English town has a well dedicated to a female saint that would once have been sacred to a healing spirit. Fairy wells are more common in England, Ireland, and Norway than they are elsewhere.

Water spirits are often described as beautiful women, though there are records of guardians taking the form of salmon, snakes, and toads. There is an ancient healing spring at Acton Barnett, in Shropshire, England, where the guardian fairies of the well appear as frogs. The largest of the three is addressed as the Dark God.

In Scotland, the Cailleach Bheur ("Blue Hag") guarded a well near the summit of Ben Cruachan, which is inclined to overflow. She had to put a slab over it every sunset and take it off every sunrise to prevent this. One evening she was so tired that she fell asleep and the water flowed down the hillside, drowning many people and beasts before forming Loch Awe. In Germany, the fairy Frau Holda's realm is reached through the bottom of a well.

Lakes, Rivers, and the Sea

Every body of water is inhabited by a spirit, or a number of spirits. Many rivers are still named after their indwelling spirit, such as the Seine in France, after Sequana; the River Severn in England, after Sabrina; the Boyne in Ireland, after Bóann; the Danube, after Danu; the Shannon, after Sinend; and so on. Names of the old spirits survive in other ways, too. On the River Trent in England, the bargees used to say that when the river was flooding, "Eager was coming." The name is derived from Aegir, the Norse sea god.

The sea is teeming with fairies such as mermaids, mermen, nymphs, and elementals, and so on. They control the weather and the water, raise storms, and have the power to cause shipwreck, drowning, and death. In ancient times, it was the practice to placate the spirits of the sea with a sacrifice before setting out on a voyage. Even today, we break a bottle of champagne over a new hull. If the sea spirits were denied their tributes, they would take another by sinking the ship and taking the souls of the sailors to dwell with them in their fabulous underwater cities. For this reason, sailors have always taken many precautions so as not to offend the spirits. They often had tattoos of nymphs, tritons, and mermaids, and would avoid saying the word *pig* or swearing while on board. If this taboo were broken, they would have to stick an iron knife in the mast to avert the ill fortune. In honour of Rân, the queen of water fairies, sailors wore a piece of gold in the form of an earring. When bad weather threatened the ship, they would throw it in the waves to placate her. She was originally a Norse goddess, the wife of Aegir.

Any body of water is an entrance to the Otherworld, and there are numerous tales of fairy kingdoms under lakes or under the sea. People frequently made offerings to the spirits that dwelt there by throwing the offering into the water. Hoards of such offerings have been found in lakes and bogs, consisting of brooches, pins, swords, shears, and so on, but all bent or broken, so that they have no use in the ordinary world, but are meant for the Otherworld.

Crossroads

Crossroads are especially magickal because they form boundaries between four roads, and consequently between the human world and Otherworld, middle earth, and the upper and lower worlds. Because of this they were dangerous places, presided over by a guardian spirit and frequented by fairies. In ancient Greece, they were sacred to Hecate, the goddess of witches. In modern Greece, a spirit called Iskios manifests at crossroads during the time of the new moon. It appears in animal form, usually a dog or a goat.

In Germany crossroads are haunted by Wod, a wild huntsman who, mounted on a white horse and accompanied by his pack of ferocious hounds, accosts lonely travellers. He spares only those who remain in the middle of the path and show no fear. These he rewards with gold and silver. (He is probably a folk survival of the god Wotan or Woden.)

In Wales, the crossroads are the domain of the banshee the Gwrach y Rhibyn ("Hag of the Dribble"), a withered crone with black teeth, tangled hair, and bat-like wings. She appears to those with relatives about to die and shrieks their names.

Croatian fairies gather at crossroads. In Rumania, the Dinsele ("They Themselves") are strange vampiric spirits that look like large cats walking on two legs. They lie at crossroads awaiting human victims in order to suck their blood, but they cannot go into the middle of the crossroads.

In France the Bon Garçons ("Good Boys") are mischievous fairies who lurk at crossroads in order to attack travellers. Occasionally one will appear in the guise of a horse, but when a person mounts it, the fairy will gallop off gleefully and finally throw the unfortunate rider into a ditch.

In ancient Rome, special spirits called *Lares Compitales* guarded boundaries (a *compita* is the marker of a boundary). At important intersections, marble altars stood with temples housing statues of two *lares* accompanied by a *genius locus* (spirit of the place). Many boundaries run along a path or road and the *lares compitales* were worshipped at both rural and urban crossroads. Sometimes they were the chief deities of a hamlet.

Crossroads were traditionally places for contacting the Otherworld. The centres of the crossroads, which were often marked by small islands of planting or a tree, literally belonged to the spirits, a no-man's-land. They were also places of execution, and gibbets stood at crossroads, as the soul of the executed man would be hurried into the underworld by the spirits. Suicides and Pagans were buried at crossroads in Christian times.

Islands

Islands are considered magickal, neither land nor sea, but places between places. Fairies live on floating islands such as the Isles of the Blest, Lochlann, the Green Meadows of Enchantment, Ynis Gwydrin, and Hy Brasil, which are only visible at certain times. Though humans have sometimes visited them, they are notoriously difficult to get to. One thing is certain: A human visitor should not offend the fairies by taking iron or steel onto the island, or removing anything from it.

In 1809, Edward Davies recorded the story of a lake near Brecknock associated with the Twyleth Teg, the Welsh fairy folk. Though an island stood in the middle of the lake it seemed small and undistinguished, but it was observed that no bird would fly over it and sometimes strains of music could be heard drifting over the water. In ancient times, a door in a nearby rock would open every May Day. Those who entered would find themselves in a passage that led to the small island, where they would be amazed to discover an enchanted garden, full of the choicest fruits and flowers, inhabited by the Twyleth Teg, whose ethereal beauty was only equalled by their courtesy and affability. Each guest would be entertained with delightful music and apprised of such future events as the fairies foresaw. The only rule was that the island was sacred, and nothing must be taken away. One day an ungrateful wretch pocketed a flower he had been presented with. This did him no good. As soon as he touched the shore, the flower vanished and he lost his senses. The Twyleth Teg were extremely angry at this sacrilege, and the door to the island has never opened from that day to this. One man tried to drain the lake to see if he could discover the fairy kingdom, but a horrible figure arose from the lake and commanded him to desist.

One of the most famous fairy islands is Avalon, which means "Isle of Apples," because the island is covered in fruitful orchards. Avalon is not just a place; it is more a state of consciousness that can be accessed when the veils that separate us from it are peeled away. It exists outside time and space. The island is inhabited by nine sisters, of which Morgan le Fay is the most beautiful and most powerful. In early Celtic legend, the island could only be reached on a boat guided by the sea god Barinthus and was a place fit only for the bravest and best. When King Arthur died, he was taken to it by four fairy queens (Morgan was one of them). There he still lies with his knights, sleeping beneath a fairy hill until Britain needs him once more.

Spirit Paths

When travelling from mound to mound, the fairies use straight pathways between them. It is unlucky for any human to build on the paths between the mounds, and people have often gone to great lengths to avoid it. When a new runway for Shannon Airport, in Ireland, was proposed, workmen refused to construct in over a fairy path.

Straight lines do not exist in nature, and have thus been considered supernatural. While nature is full of curves and bends, the straight is Otherworldly, associated with gods, spirits, fairies, and ghosts. In many places, it is believed that spirits travel in straight lines. It is widely believed that the dead must travel by the shortest route and in a straight line. In China, bad spirits travel on straight paths, so it is thought that straight paths are dangerous for humans.

Though the theory of ley lines is usually dated to Alfred Watkins (1921), straight lines known as fairy paths or ghost roads were spoken of for several centuries prior. An Irish seer told Evans Wentz in 1911 that fairy paths were lines of energy that circulates the Earth's magnetism. While the straight alignments between ancient sites were only noted by scholars in the 18th century, tales of these straight fairy paths were current among the peasantry since time immemorial.

Labyrinths

Fairies are said to dwell in the various labyrinths of England. Labyrinths were ritual pathways used to retrieve the spring from the underworld, which lay at its centre, to revive the souls of the dead, and to perform weather magick.[2]

Stone Circles and Standing Stones

Wherever stone circles and standing stones exist, they have been connected with fairies. The Channel Isles were once thought to be fairy islands, because of the many prehistoric graves, stone circles, and monuments there. Locals believed that they had been built by *Les Petits Faîtiaux* (the fairies) to live in. The prehistoric sites themselves were sometimes called *pouquelaie* or "fairy dwellings."

The beings that inhabit sacred sites are as old as time; they protect the holy places. In Brittany, for example, they are called the Korred and guard the ancient dolmens and the treasures that lie beneath them. They are said to have large heads, red eyes, dark skin, hairy bodies, spiky hair, cloven feet, sharp noses, spindly arms and legs, and cat's claws. As the summer is ushered in at the start of May, you may find traces of their wild dances, which leave burnt circles in the grass.

In Cornwall, in Southwest England, the guardian fairies are called Spriggans ("Spirits"). They keep treasure beneath the old stones. One night a man tried to dig up the treasure buried under Trencrom Hill. As he neared the gold all about him went dark, thunder crashed and lightening streaked the sky. By its light, he saw a large number of Spriggans swarming out of the rocks. At first they were small, but they soon swelled in size until they were as big as giants. The man managed to escape, but without his treasure. He was so shaken by his experience that he took to his bed and never worked again.

Wreaths of eerie mist often surround the stone circles. Should you find a gap in the mist you will be able to pass through into the Otherworld. This is more likely at the magickal "times between times" of May Day, Halloween, or the Midsummer Solstice.

Forests

The grove was the centre of Celtic religion, the place where spirits were contacted, and the forest is alive with the chattering of the Otherworld, where messages can be heard in the whistling wind and the whispering of the leaves in the trees.

Vast numbers of fairies dwell in the forests. In Croatia, for example, the Sumske Dekle ("Woodland Maidens") are fairy girls, covered in hair. When humans leave food out for them they will return the favour by cleaning their houses. In Greece, the Sylvans are beautiful but dangerous, sometimes luring travellers to their deaths in the forests. In Hungarian fairy lore, the Vadleany ("Forest Girl") appears as a naked woman with hair so long that it sweeps the ground. When the forest rustles, it tells of her presence.

Among the Southern and Western Slavs, the Vile ("Whirlwind") dwell in woodlands and ride about them on horses or on stags, hunting deer with their arrows and herding chamois. Some of the forest Vily are connected with particular trees in the manner of dryads and cannot venture far from them. In Dalmatia, they are described as the troop of Herodias, the witch queen. In Serbia they are called *divna* "the divine," and it seems likely that they were originally Pagan goddesses, later associated with witch lore.

In both the orient and the occident, there are tales of spirits such as elves and pixies who inhabit trees. According to popular lore it is bad luck to cut down a tree, particularly those associated with fairies, such as hawthorn, oak, birch, and rowan. The Arabian Djinn sometimes live in trees; in ancient Greece and Rome forests were the home of Dryads, Pans, and Centaurs, among others. Various nymphs were associated with particular trees, such as Rhoea with the pomegranate, Daphne with the laurel, and Helike with the willow. In Scandinavia and Germany, the forest spirits are often wild people covered in moss, or Moss Maidens.

Fairy Rings

These appear as bright green rings on the grass, or more likely a circle of fairy ring mushrooms (*Marasmius oreades*), which materialize on lawns and in meadows, leaving a circular bare patch or later in the year a brighter patch of grass. They are said to be a favourite dancing place of the fairies. It is now thought that some of these rings are as many as 600 years old.

Be warned, though: If you should join the fairies in their revels, you may become invisible to your companions outside the ring and find that it is impossible to leave, and be forced to dance until you collapse and die of exhaustion. Some have found that an evening spent in a fairy ring turns out to be many years in the human realm.

A story from the Vale of Neath, in Wales, relates that Rhys and Llewelyn were travelling home one day in the twilight, when Rhys called to his companion to stop and listen to the music. It was a tune, he said, to which he had danced a hundred times, and he must go and dance now. Llewelyn could hear nothing, and began to remonstrate. But Rhys darted away, and he called after him in vain. Accordingly he went home, put up the ponies, ate his supper, and went to bed, thinking that Rhys had only made a pretext for going to the alehouse. But when morning came, and there was still no sign of Rhys, he told his master what had occurred. A search proved fruitless, and suspicion fell on Llewelyn of having murdered his friend, and he was put in jail.

However, a farmer in the neighbourhood, skilled in fairy matters, guessed what had really happened and proposed that several people should accompany Llewelyn to the place where he parted with Rhys. Upon coming to it, Llewellyn called out that he could hear music. All listened, but could hear nothing. But Llewelyn's foot was on the outward edge of the fairy-ring. "Put your foot on mine, David," he said to the man standing near him. The latter did so, and so did each of the party, one after the other, and then all of them heard the sound of many harps, and saw within the circle, about 20 feet across, great numbers of little people dancing round and round. Among them was Rhys, whom Llewelyn caught by the smock, as he came by him, and pulled him out of the circle. Rhys urged him to go home and let him finish his dance, because he had only been dancing for five minutes. It was only by force they got him away; and he could not be persuaded of the time that had passed in the dance.

Mounds

Entrances to Fairyland are often said to be through mounds, which occasionally open at the knocking of a witch, or at certain times of year, such as Halloween and May Day. These burial chambers, dating from the Neolithic period onwards, are found throughout Europe. There are upwards of 40,000 in Britain alone. They vary in size from a few feet across to more than 300 feet in diameter. From Scandinavian to Celtic, Germanic and Slavonic lore, earth mounds are described as occasionally glowing or giving off a strange light.

Mounds are a link between the living and the dead, this world and the next. Both Saxons and Celts thought that fairies lived in mounds. Fairy mounds are also sometimes called "Dane Forts," probably from *dun*, meaning a hill, as in dune, or from the Scandinavian *dáin*, meaning "dead," referring to a spirit or ghost. Hill elves were known in Anglo-Saxon writings as *dunaelfen*. The name of the Dane Hills in Leicestershire, England—where the hag or witch Black Annis lives—probably has the same origin. Again, it may be that *dane* derives from the Celtic goddess Danu, widely known as the mother of the fairies.

The ghosts of the dead were widely believed to dwell in an underworld kingdom, along with the fairies, ruled by the Lord of the Dead, the Fairy King. In South Wales he is called Gwyn ap Nudd and rules the Welsh fairies the Twyleth Teg. The entrance to his kingdom is through the Welsh lakes, or beneath Glastonbury Tor in England. In North Wales the King of the Fairies is Arawn, an ancient Welsh god of the underworld. In one story, he changed places with the human King Pwyll for a time. In Ulster myth, he is Finvarra ("White-topped"), King of the Daoine Sidhe of the west or Connacht, living in the mound of Meadha. Finvarra was once a god of the dead and underworld, with some functions as a vegetation spirit because he is deemed to have the power of bringing good harvests.

Many burial mounds (such as artificial earth wombs) are orientated so that the shaft of the sun, at the Winter Solstice, will strike a point in the underground chamber and trigger the rebirth of the sun, along with the ancestral spirits entombed there. Moreover, the dead had all the ancestral knowledge. Witches went to the underworld to converse with them and learn spells. For ordinary people, this journey was very risky.

To find the entrance to a fairy hill you should walk nine times around the hill.

Caves

Like burial mounds, caves are entrances to the underworld, long associated with spirits including a great
many fairies, the best known being the dwarfs. They mine
precious stones and metals, guard the earth and its riches,
and are spirits of rocks and caverns. Dwarfs live within
the Scandinavian and German mountains. They move easily through the earth and are masters of all its minerals.
Though people used to have friendly relations with the
dwarfs, they are rarely seen now.

A young girl left a hayfield in the Lavantthal,
Carinthia, to climb the Schönofen, where there is a fine
view over the valley. As she reached the top she became
aware of an open door in the rock. She entered and found
herself in a cellar-like room. Two fine black steeds stood
at the fodder-trough and fed off the finest oats. Marvel-
ling how they got there, she put a few handfuls of the
oats into her pocket and passed on into a second chamber. A chest stood there, and on the chest lay a black
dog. Near him was a loaf of bread, in which a knife was
stuck. With ready wit she divined the purpose of the
bread; and cutting a good slice she threw it to the dog.
While he was busy devouring it she filled her apron from
the treasure contained in the chest. But meantime the
door closed, and there was nothing for it but to lie down
and sleep. She awoke to find the door wide open, and at
once made the best of her way home, but she was not a
little astounded to learn that she had been gone for a
whole year.

Caves were the first temples of ancient man, who saw
any entrance into the Earth as an opening into the fecund
womb of Mother Earth.

Rainbows

The leprechaun's pot of gold is found at the end of the rainbow. If you have ever tried to stand at the end of a rainbow, you will know that it is a place that cannot be reached physically, but only in spirit. For this reason, the rainbow is often thought to be the bridge to the world of the gods, the afterlife, or Fairyland. The Anglo Saxons believed that the Earth and Otherworld of the gods was connected by the Rainbow Bridge Bifrost, the Trembling Way of fire.

Mountains

Mountains are powerful places, where people often felt that approached the realm of the gods and spirits. Particular mountains were considered especially sacred, and some are still revered to this day. Mountains are the dwelling places of numerous fairies, including the Bohemian Herr Johannes, who lives on the wooded slopes of the Reisengebirge and is known as the Master of the Mountains. Alpine fairies called the Salvanelli are merry fellows who love to play tricks, misleading travellers and leaving them stranded on high mountain ledges. Among the Slavs, the Samogorska inhabits the high peaks and hilltops. The Tennin are lovely fairy maidens of Buddhist lore, sometimes encountered on the highest summit of the mountains. In Slovenia the Vesna live in mountain palaces and influence the fates of both men and crops. Fairies were often encountered on the high mountain passes, and shrines were sometimes placed there.

-------- THE PERILS OF FAIRYLAND --------

To encounter the world of fairies, you must first realize that the whole world and everything in it is alive, animate,
conscious, and infused with spirit. It is sacred and holy. This
includes trees, rocks, stones, animals, even city streets, and
hearth fires. It is a wonderful and exciting feeling to compre-
hend this, but one that brings with it responsibilities. The
Walker between the Worlds has duties and obligations. Visits to Fairyland are fraught with danger. Once you have
entered the fairy world, nothing will ever be the same again.
Fairy lore is full of warnings about people who have visited
Fairyland and ever afterwards pined for its glory.

Time flows differently in the Otherworld, and humans
who think they have passed a single year with the fairies
may return to their homes to find them ruined by time, and
their friends and relatives aged or long dead and buried.
One such was Oisin, the son of Finn Mac Cool, chief of the
Fenian warriors of Ireland. He was hunting one day when a
fairy woman called Niamh of the Golden Hair approached
him. She had chosen him for her lover and together they
journeyed to the fairyland. After 300 years he expressed a
wish to see his home and she lent him a fairy horse, with the
caution not to let his feet touch the earth. He was dismayed
to see that all had changed. Even the men seemed feebler.
He saw three trying to move a rock and as he lent down to
give them a hand his saddle girth suddenly snapped and he
fell to the earth. The horse vanished and he instantly
became ancient and blind.

Near Bridgend (South Wales) is a place where a woman is
said to have lived who was absent 10 years with the fairies, and
thought she was not out of the house more than 10 minutes.

With a woman's proverbial persistency, she would not believe her husband's assurances that it was 10 years since she disappeared.

Alternatively, a person may think that he has spent many years in Fairyland, but has been absent from the mundane world for only a few minutes. This occurred in the case of the Pembrokeshire shepherd, who joined a dance in a fairy ring and found himself in the Otherworld. He lived happily for several years among the fairies, feasting and drinking with them in their lovely palaces. However, he was warned that he must not drink from a magickal fountain that stood in the centre of the gardens. Inevitably, he eventually broke the taboo and plunged into the water. He instantly found himself back on the hillside, with his flock of sheep, having been absent for only a few moments of ordinary time.

These distortions in time are experienced by anyone who visits the Otherworld, whether in meditation or through ritual, or some other discipline. When, as a witch, I cast a circle, I create a place that exists between the worlds. The circle is not a barrier to keep things out, or a container to keep the power in, it is an interface between the worlds, where all the worlds can be accessed. We sometime think that we have spent an hour or two inside the circle, when six or seven hours have passed in the everyday world.

The old shamans took power plants, which enabled the sight and caused time distortions. Some think this is why fairies have so many associations with the white-spotted red fly agaric mushrooms (*Amanita muscaria*), which is psychotropic and has a long history of use among European mystics. The effects of the mushroom include auditory and visual hallucinations and spatial distortions. Subjects commonly report sensations of flying, or seeing little people or red-hatted mushrooms dancing. Fly agaric grows under birch trees and the Siberian shaman's seven-stepped pole was made of birch. In other words, the shaman ingested the mushroom and flew up the *cosmic axis* tree to the spirit realms, seeing the tutelary spirit of the agaric as a red-capped fairy. (Note: This mushroom is deadly poisonous. Shamans used to drink the urine of reindeer, which had eaten the mushrooms with impunity and thus removed all the more harmful compounds, which lead to vomiting, paralysis, and death.)

A number of legends speak of one-eyed, one-legged creatures, and these may, in fact, be a code for psychotropic mushrooms. The fachan, a Highland fairy, has one eye, one hand, one leg, one ear, one arm, and one toe all lined up down the centre of his body. He carries a spiked club with which he attacks any human who dares to approach his mountain realm. He hates all living creatures but especially birds, which he envies for their gift of flight. A number of writers have theorizsed that the fachan may be a folk memory of the Celtic shamans, who stood on one leg and closed one eye when casting spells. The usual explanation offered for this practice is so that one eye looks into the inner realms, and only standing on one leg symbolizes not being wholly in one realm or another. However, it may be that the stance is in imitation of the mushroom that gives the shaman his power, the one-legged, one-eyed fly agaric. The fact that the fachan inhabits a mountainous region is significant, as that is where the fly agaric grows. His hatred of birds, which he envies for their flight, may be a distorted folk memory of the gift of flight the mushroom bestows.

There was also an Irish race of one-legged, one-eyed beings described as the oldest inhabitants of the land, a race of wizards who intermarried with the Tuatha Dé Danaan. In Celtic lore, all red food was taboo, including rowan berries and red nuts. These may be masks for the mushroom in Irish myth, adding that the Celts were head hunters, believing that all wisdom and power resided in the head. Perhaps these heads were not only human ones but also the heads of vision giving mushrooms.

The Father Christmas costume of white and red also suggests the mushroom. Siberian winter dwellings were excavated holes with a birch log roofs; the only entrance was through a smoke hole in the roof. Even the summer dwellings had smoke-hole exits for the spirit of the shaman to fly out of when he was in a trance. This might explain why Santa enters and exits through the chimney. Why does Santa bring gifts? The shaman is the middleman between humans and spirits and brings back knowledge from the spirit world. Ordinary individuals would write requests on pieces of paper and burn them, so their messages would be carried to the spirits on the smoke.

Fairy food, which is generally described as being red in colour, is prohibited for humans. Should they eat it, they can never return to the realm of men. This is comparable with the taboos placed on shamanic substances forbidding them to ordinary men and women. Among the Selkup, fly agaric was believed to be fatal to non-shamans. Among the Vogul, consumption was limited to sacred occasions and it was abused on peril of death. The Indo-Europeans strictly limited the important ritual of soma to certain classes and the profane user risked death at the hands of the angry god. Amongst the Celts, red foods and mushrooms were taboo, designated as the food of the Otherworld or the dead. As the mushroom aids the shaman to visit other realms in spirit flight, see spirits, and contact the spirit or god within, Robert Graves[3] argued that ambrosia, the food of the gods, was in reality hallucinogenic mushrooms.

Descriptions of visits to Fairyland might easily describe a drug-induced visionary experience—enhanced colours, unearthly music, spatial distortions, the loss of any sense of the passage of time, and food and drink tasting wonderful. However, when the traveller returns (or the vision ends) fairy gold turns to withered leaves or common rubbish.

Fairies are said to dwell in mounds, in caves, or underground in general, and a common shamanic experience is the visit to the underworld. Shamans and witches are said to receive their powers from spirits or fairies. Fairies can confer gifts of healing and magick and prophecy.

3

Techniques for Fairy Contact

airies are a link between the world of humans and the world of spirit, flitting between the two realms, though only rarely perceived by our grosser vision. It should be remembered that the sight of fairies is often an inner one, not a physical experience. Fairies are usually encountered during meditation, in visions and in dreams; imagination is one of the main doorways we can use to access the Otherworld.

However, occasionally you may catch glimpses of them in the physical realm, as fleeting shapes or balls of coloured light. You may hear the sounds of laughter, piping, or the harp, or detect an unexplained musky scent. Full manifestation is very rare, though it does happen. In these cases, the spirits are usually very pale and shining, perhaps in humanoid form, though they can take any shape they wish; their appearance is a glamour. They may appear as people, animals, plants, and even flames. We do not see their true form, and in all probability any two people witnessing a manifestation may see the creature differently. It may be that the shapes fairies assume are for our benefit, or it may be that the contour we see is merely the mind's attempt to make sense of an unfamiliar image.

The Otherworld has a habit of breaking through into this world to contact us, if only we have the eyes to see it and the ears to hear it. If you approach a numinous place with an open heart and heightened awareness, you may be astonished at what you experience. There are a wide variety of exercises you can follow to help make you more aware, and some of them are detailed in this chapter, but Nature herself is the greatest teacher in this quest.

Contact from the Otherworld may be spontaneous and surprising. You may become aware of synchronicities—things that seem coincidental but are not. You may come across a piece of information that answers your immediate questions, a book that comes to hand containing knowledge that you need, and so on. You might become aware that the same bird greets you each morning and reappears throughout the day for several weeks. These types of omens are very individual, and you won't find them in any dictionary of dreams or divination. It is important not to over-analyze them and look for related symbolism, because fairies rarely use symbolism to communicate with us. Their messages usually mean "look at what I'm showing you" or "listen to what I am telling you." Contact with fairy powers may trigger all sorts of memories, abilities, and understanding that you never knew you had. You may be fairy-led on our journeys, taken from the worn path on to a new way. You may feel lost at first, but you will arrive at the place you most need to be.

Fairies have their own courses and objectives; their reason for existence is not to be your teacher, and they

are certainly not there for your entertainment. Any friendship with fairies is on their terms, and offending them will
have dire consequences. It should be remembered that
there are both munificent fairies and malevolent fairies.
Both kinds demand a price for their assistance. If the help
required maintains the balance of the universe, all's well
and good; if it doesn't, it creates an imbalance that most
certainly will eventually lead to the downfall of the magician. A fairy will not have any association with a greedy
person, a selfish person, a polluter of the environment, a
harmer of other people or other creatures, except in
order to trick and punish them.

However, there have always been fairy workers, and
some fairies still seek to work with humans in order to try
to restore the natural balance to the world, and prevent its
slow destruction by environmental poison and pollution.

——TRAVELLING BETWEEN THE REALMS——

In the fairy legends, there are many tales of people
travelling to the Otherworld to speak with its denizens.
Sometimes a person will encounter a fairy and be conveyed there by them, as in the story of Thomas the Rhymer.
They may encounter one of the places where Fairyland
and the human world meet, like a fairy ring. Sometimes
they will chase a strange animal into Fairyland, as in the
tale of the mysterious white hart that led King Arthur
through a cave to Morgan le Fay's palace, where he was shown
the heavens and the Earth. Some have ridden fairy horses
into the Otherworld, such as the Irish hero Conan, who was
carried there by the horse Aonbharr. Thomas the Rhymer
was taken to the realm of the fairy by the milk-white steed of

the Elf Queen, and Tam Lin escaped from Fairyland on a stolen white horse.

If we read between the lines of these stories, to the heart of the spiritual truth they contain, the horse is a metaphor for the method that conveys the seer into Otherworld consciousness. A shaman's drum is often referred to as his "horse," because the drumbeat is the method that helps him induce a trance that enables him to attain Otherworld consciousness. The horse spirit carries the shaman into other realms. It is said that the shaman tethers his horse to the World Tree, a mythical cosmic axis that links the three realms: Earth, where we live; the heavens, where the gods live; and the underworld, where the fairies live.

In Celtic myth, the horse goddess Epona ("Pony") carries a key that unlocked both the stable door and the gates of the Otherworld. She rides between the worlds at will, to carry souls to the afterlife on horseback, accompanied by blackbirds and larks. She is also a shamanic deity, who carries the seer or bard to the Otherworld. She is, in fact, the Fairy Queen who travels between the realms on her white horse. In Wales, she was called Rhiannon, whose seven blackbirds called dreamers into Fairyland.

In Greek myth, the horse of Otherworld journeying was Pegasos (Latin Pegasus) who was the horse of Apollo and the Muses, and the inspiration of poetry. On Mount Helicon, there was a spring called Hippocrene ("the Horse Well"), which was horse-shoe shaped and was said to have been made when Pegasus ("of the springs of water") stamped there; poets drank its waters for inspiration. If a poet said, "I am mounting my Pegasus," he meant that he was inspired to write poetry. Poetry and bardship was a serious business, not mere rhyme-making. It meant being given divine inspiration from the Otherworld. Many famous poets and musicians are said to have learned their crafts in the Otherworld or the realm of the fairy.

Some people have entered the Otherworld by eating its food. These stories reflect shamanic practices throughout the world. The ancient Celts, among others, had a taboo on eating red food, which was believed to belong to the fairies or to the ghosts of the dead. Its use was confined to shamans and to feasts of the dead. This recalls the taboo nature of fairy food, which humans are forbidden to eat or they will not be able to leave Fairyland.

SHUTTING OFF THE WORLD

It is a fact that although children are often aware of fairy folk, most people lose contact as they get older. The cares and stresses of the everyday world intrude; we get caught up in other things. The Otherworld may be trying to communicate with you, but cannot get through the babble of *"What shall I make for dinner? What shall I wear tonight? I must get my suit from the dry cleaners?"* and so on. We must be able to slow down and listen to the rhythms of Elphame.

Sometimes the Otherworld forces us to do this. One of the ways it uses is to make us too ill to have any interaction with the outside world. In illness we stop trying to achieve and simply learn to exist, to *be*. In the ensuing quiet, the world of spirits opens. This is the basis of the shamanic initiation. Sometimes tribal shamans have been subject to natural illnesses during which the spirits speak to them, and sometimes the crisis is provoked with drugs and arduous physical practices.

I underwent a shamanic initiation through illness some time ago. I became sick to the point where I was confined to bed for nearly two years. I felt that I was separated from the world of humankind; it seemed to me that humans were like the creatures on the surface of a pond, skittering here and there in the glittering light, darting hurriedly through life. On the other hand, the pace of my life became slower and slower, and, as it did, I sank further and further down into the great pond, until I lay at the bottom, in the gloom of the thick mud, where I could see the roots of things. I witnessed how everything was generated in the darkness and grew toward the light. I saw the creative cauldron of the Universe. The fast-moving people on the surface never saw this; they were too busy and bound up with solely with their own concerns.

Trees live for centuries, and to them we seem to pass in a blur, but during my illness I had slowed down to the point where it became easy to talk to plant and tree spirits, though almost impossible for me to communicate with other people.

You will never contact the wildfolk while your mind is cluttered with the business of everyday life. To work with fairies you have to learn to shut out the prattle of the human world and the inner chatter of your mind. When you find the still, silent place within, the Otherworld can begin to communicate with you. Don't rush, don't try to force it, stop trying to accomplish it, and simply learn to *be*.

Meditation helps in this aim; it develops mental clarity, and imagination is the greatest tool we posses when working with spiritual disciplines. You may use meditation and pathworking as the first step in recovering lost levels of consciousness, to clear the mind and even establish contact with the Otherworld. When you relax your body, it is easier to relax your mind, to slow down the rapid fire of surface thoughts and access deeper levels of awareness.

——STOPPING THE INTERNAL DIALOGUE——

Have you noticed that you are constantly talking to yourself inside your mind? This constant dialogue of the logical left brain with the ego prevents other levels of consciousness from becoming apparent, and reinforces the existing state of perceptions of the world. You must learn to stop this "internal dialogue" still the mind, empty it in order to become aware of greater levels of consciousness, and to develop clairvoyant and other psychic facilities.

Light a candle and gaze at the flame. Try to empty your mind of all thoughts and let it be clear and still. This is very difficult. If you find thoughts creeping in, gently push them away, and re-centre your concentration on the candle flame. Try to do this exercise for five minutes a day. You could try doing it by concentrating on any object; it doesn't have to be a candle flame. And so, for example, you could do it on the bus to work, or sitting in the park at lunchtime. When you have progressed, do the exercise with your eyes open or closed, not looking at any object in particular.

This is probably the most important exercise you will do, so don't shirk it. It becomes easier, and you will find that it has great benefits. You will become calmer, less stressed, and your perceptions will become clearer.

PATHWORKING

Pathworking, or guided meditation, is a tool used by mystics to foster spiritual development, to open the psychic senses, and to visit all the realms of the Otherworld. After a time, the pathworker begins to realize that the landscapes and persons met do not all belong to his or her internal world, but constitute messages and lessons from the Otherworld. In time, he or she will also learn to recognize spiritual lessons manifesting in the physical realm, because the realms coexist in the same space.

The pathworkings given here consist of three parts. The first stage is the relaxation stage, and to avoid onerous repetition, the instruction given for this is "relax." This means the whole of the relaxation exercise in this chapter should be gone through. Then is the pathworking proper. The third stage is the awakening stage, given at the end of each pathworking as "return yourself to waking consciousness," but meaning that the awakening exercise given in this chapter should be gone through each time.

Preparing to Meditate

At first you may find pathworking difficult. You will itch and want to fidget, or find that you can't concentrate. Many people have problems with visualization at first. The trick is to make sure your body is completely relaxed and allow yourself to drift into it. Don't try too hard—this is

counter-productive. Once you have experienced the pleasant feeling of deep relaxation you will find it easier to
achieve it a second time. The next time will be even easier.
I have taught pathworking meditation for more than 20
years and I have never found anyone who was incapable of
using the method.

The relaxation technique that follows is the one I
always use, counting people down into relaxation and walking them down five imaginary steps into the pathworking.
There are many other methods, and some teachers will
ask their students to imagine themselves going down an
escalator, climbing up steps, and so on. It doesn't really
matter as long as the meditators can relate to the imagery,
but I find it that helps if the same method is used every
time. The words and images act as an instant mental trigger. As soon as I begin talking, my students know what is
coming. After many sessions with someone, all I have to
say is "lie down and relax," and he or she is already in a
meditative state.

A good pathworking is not too detailed. It will take
the meditator into a place or situation, and then leave him
or her plenty of time to look around and experience what
he or she needs to. Any pathworking that charts each step
and image is merely showing you what the author imag-
ines, not what is true for you. You might as well just read
a short story—this is not meditation!

After a pathworking, write down as much of it as you
can remember, in as much detail as possible. You will find
that some of it fades like a dream. As you progress and
continue to record your experiences, you may discover
that the small details that seemed insignificant were, with
hindsight, very important.

Relaxation Before Pathworking

Remember that during a pathworking a narrator helps you to enter a state of relaxation, and then relates an imaginary scene. After the experience is over, the narrator helps you to bring yourself back to waking consciousness. You are not under someone else's control, just deeply relaxed, and you can stop and return to ordinary waking consciousness whenever you like. If you wish, you can record the narration yourself on tape, and play the tape each time.

Find a comfortable, warm space where you can be undisturbed. Take the phone off the hook. You might like to lie down on the floor with a cushion under your head, on your bed, or sit upright on a comfortable chair. Lie or sit comfortably, arms and legs uncrossed, and allow all your muscles to relax.

Concentrate on your breathing; with each breath, you become more and more relaxed. With each outward breath you let go of tensions, you let go of the events of the day; you let go of problems.

Centre your attention on your toes, be fully aware of them, and let them relax.

Move your attention to the soles of your feet, be fully aware of them, and let them relax; feel the tension drain away.

Move slowly in the same way through the tops of your feet, your ankles, your shins and calves, your knees, your thighs, your bottom, your stomach, your spine (feel each vertebrae separate and relax), your chest (be aware that your breathing has become slow and rhythmical), your shoulders, your arms and elbows, your hands and fingers, your neck, your scalp, your face. Feel the muscles of your forehead relax, the muscles around your eyes, your nose, mouth, cheeks, jaw.

Concentrate again on your breathing. With each breath you become more and more relaxed. With each breath, you go deeper and deeper into a warm, pleasant state of relaxation.

Now imagine that you are at the top of a flight of five steps, leading downward. As you go down each step, in turn you will go deeper and deeper into relaxation. Go down one step at a time, noticing what the steps are made of, how they feel. Five...four...three...two...one....(Now continue with the pathworking chosen.)

Returning From the Pathworking

When you are ready to return, walk back the way you came until you reach the flight of five steps.

As you ascend each step, you become more and more awake, more conscious of your body and the room in which you are sitting or lying, until at the fifth step you are completely awake. One...two...three... four...five.... Slowly open your eyes and stretch.

You may be surprised at how long you spent in your meditational state. What seemed to be 10 minutes may have turned out to be an hour in real time. In meditation, time and space become irrelevant. As soon as you can, write down what you experienced during your meditation, including as many details as possible.

Journey to Avalon Pathworking

Imagine that you are standing on the edge of a lake. An eerie mist covers the water and you cannot see more than a few yards. Even the birds are quiet.

You become aware of the sound of a gentle splashing. Slowly a stately barge glides into view. It crests through the water as if by magick and comes to rest on the shore before you. It is made of silver and has a moon-white sail. In it sits a noble-looking woman, clad all in red. Her hair is also red, and flows long and sleek down her back. She holds out her hand to you, and you step into the boat.

The barge starts to move silently through the gossamer threads of mist that shroud the lake. Your companion is quiet, but smiles gently at you.

Eventually your magick barge comes to rest beside a jetty made from some snow-white wood, and you step ashore to find yourself on an enchanted island. Though the mists hide it from the mortal world, the island is lit by bright sunshine. It is covered by orchards of apple trees, which bear drifts of blossom, which the gentle breeze scatters, creating a snowstorm of soft petals. Among the branches also hang mature fruit, round golden apples, full and ripe.

Morgan le Fay—for your hostess is none other—bids you welcome to her realm. You may stay here as long as you like, speaking with Morgan le Fay. She knows all the secrets of magick and herbs, and may share some of these with you.

When you are ready to return, thank your hostess and take the magick barge back to the shore of the human realm.

Crossing the Rainbow Bridge Pathworking

You stand before a great gorge, a chasm that separates the world of humans from the Otherworld of the fairies. Spanning the gulf is a rainbow bridge, shimmering in the light.

The end of the bridge sweeps down to your feet. You realize that it is possible to cross this bridge into Fairyland.

You step forward and enter the red band of the rainbow. A soft, red light bathes you. It is the colour of life...of vigour...of strength. You are drifting safely and gently upwards. You drift gently up into...

...a soft, orange light. Orange light bathes you. It is the colour of confidence...of daring...of ecstasy...of joy. You are drifting safely and gently upwards. You drift gently up into...

...a soft, yellow light. Yellow light bathes you. It is the colour of mental power...of lucidity of mind. You are drifting safely and gently upwards. You drift gently up into...

...a soft, green light. Green light bathes you. It is the colour of increase...of inventiveness. You are drifting safely and gently upwards. You drift gently up into...

...a soft, blue light. Blue light bathes you. It is the colour of healing...of truth...of defense. You

are drifting safely and gently upwards. You drift gently up into...

...a band of violet light. Violet light bathes you. It is the colour of majesty...of insight...of spiritual healing. You are drifting safely and gently upwards. You drift gently up into...

...clear indigo light, which frames the gate of Otherworld. It is up to you whether you go on or go back now. If the time is right, many secrets will be shown to you in the Otherworld, but if this is not the right time, you should go back and be thankful for what you have already been shown.

Whether you want to go back now or later, you must return through the layers of the Rainbow Bridge: indigo...violet...blue...green...yellow...orange... red. Finally, you find yourself back on earth.

Return to waking consciousness.

The Hollow Oak Pathworking

Relax.

It is Midsummer Eve. The sky is clear and studded with stars. You find yourself in a primeval forest, alive with the power of magick.

You begin to follow an ancient pathway, which leads you to a clearing.

In the centre stands a massive oak tree. It is the king of the forest, colossal, centuries old. The branches spread like a leafy canopy above, while you know that its roots extend as wide below ground.

The oak is a magickal cosmic axis, linking all the realms of existence, from the human world where you stand, to the upper world of the gods and spirits, and the underworld of the fairies.

The oak is hollow, and you squeeze yourself inside a natural doorway into the warm trunk.

The oak stands at the boundary of the year, between the time of the waxing sun and the time of the waning sun. You can feel the year turning, and the gates between the worlds opening.

You burrow down inside the hollow oak, and a passageway deep into the Earth opens up before you. The way is lit by tiny lanterns.

Gradually, as you walk downwards, you begin to make out the sound of music, a beautiful, haunting tune, played on harp and pipes. As you travel further, it gets louder, and you are aware of lights ahead.

You emerge from the passageway into a bright hall, full of dazzling fairy folk. They are beautiful, slender, tall, with shining pale skin and white robes. They are laughing and feasting at tables heavily laden with food and wine.

They become aware of your presence and greet you with delight.

You feel yourself being led through the hall towards a pair of golden thrones. On them, sit the Fairy King and Queen. You bow before them courteously.

The Fairy Queen takes an apple from the low silver table at her side and offers it to you.

As you reach for it, she warns you sternly, "Know that if you eat of this Otherworldly fruit, you will be changed forever. You will be part human and part fairy, and your path will be difficult and often painful. When you are away from the Otherworld you will long for it, but when you return to us the sweetness of this realm is almost unbearable."

You may eat, or decline politely. The choice is yours alone.

You can spend some time among the fairies now, and speak to them as you wish; they may answer your questions, if they like you.

When it seems time for you to leave, say your goodbyes, and remember that you can take nothing away from Fairyland.

You return to the underground passage, and travel up it into the hollow oak.

You realise that the sun has risen, and you feel the warmth on your skin.

Return yourself to waking consciousness.

The Birds of Rhiannon Pathworking

Relax.

You find yourself in a beautiful meadow at dawn. A white mist rises from the ground, which is heavy with dew.

There is a dawn chorus of birdsong surrounding you.

As the light grows, you realize that the number of birds singing is becoming fewer. More and more birds fall silent.

At last, only a few voices remain—all blackbirds. Then these, too, stop.

In the eerie silence that has fallen, the mist thickens until it blots out your view of the meadow. It surrounds you completely like a translucent pearl, so that you cannot see which direction you face.

Slowly, a parting forms in the mist, and you see dark shapes ahead of you— seven blackbirds.

They flutter in front of you and seem to want to lead you on, now and again landing to wait for you.

You follow them through the gap in the mist.

You emerge into a meadow that seems very much like the one you just left, but it is much brighter, the sunlight is warmer and more golden. The grass is greener, the flowers more vibrant, and the trees that surround it are apple trees, heavy with pink and white blossoms, and round red fruit.

You hear the sound of a harp drifting from beyond the trees, thrilling and enchanting you.

You move toward it.

Beyond the line of apple trees is a magickal sight. Silken pavilions have been erected around a field; before each is planted a heraldic standard, depicting various animals and symbols. There are white horses, harts, boars, badgers, and so on.

Around these pavilions, warriors, clad in gold and silver armour, ride on horseback. Brilliantly dressed men and women stroll about, talking and laughing. They are all very tall and slender, pale-skinned, and seeming to have some inner luminosity. These are the wildfolk.

You walk towards them and they notice you.

A beautiful lady comes forward to greet you. She is dressed entirely in green, and her emerald eyes twinkle with merriment.

She takes you by the hand and leads you into the grandest of the pavilions, a marvellous arabesque structure of saffron silk, hung with multi-coloured pennants that flutter in the breeze. The standard before it shows seven blackbirds.

Inside the tent is the Fairy Queen, Rhiannon, the rider between the worlds. She is seated on a crystal throne, on the back of which her seven blackbirds are perched. Her dress is made of gossamer strands and seems to sparkle as if with diamonds, but they are drops of dew scattered upon it. Her long golden hair is spread about her.

You kneel and make your greeting.

She smiles and bids you welcome.

You may spend time now in the Otherworld with the Fairy Queen—if she wishes it—or wandering about the festive gathering. You may speak to the others, if they are willing.

When you are ready to return, make your goodbyes.

The blackbirds lead you back across the meadow to where the mist still hangs.

Go through the mist and find yourself back in the everyday world.

When you are ready, return yourself to waking consciousness.

Dreaming With The Eyes Open

If you are merely an observer, you will never make contact with fairies; you must knowingly interact with the landscape. I don't mean you have to be a farmer or gardener, or move out of the city, but you must approach landscape with enhanced sensitivity. Sometimes we call this light trance consciousness "dreaming with the eyes open."

To achieve it, when you first arrive at a place, greet it as you would a living being. Stand or sit quietly for a while. Try to relax your body as you would for a pathworking. Still your mind by closing your eyes and concentrating on the sounds around you, perhaps you can hear the birds and the wind, or the rolling of the sea on the shore. Be aware of your mind probing around the area, seeking its ambience, its energies, and its places of interaction with the Otherworld.

Then open your eyes. While maintaining this heightened consciousness, you can walk though the place and explore it with new levels of awareness.

The Witch Walk

The Witch Walk is a pilgrimage that relies on the Otherworld to give you direction. To begin, dedicate the journey to the higher powers, and ask that you will be guided. Put yourself in the light trance state called *dreaming with the eyes open*. Now ask the spirits to direct your footsteps (or your driving), turning right or left as they dictate. Sometimes, you will feel the direction as a magnetic pull; at other times, as a heat on your face. Sometimes the Otherworld will send messengers in the form of birds, animals, or butterflies to lead the way. Treat everything that happens to you on a Witch Walk as significant, whether this is a person or animal that you meet, a place or plant you discover, and so on.

When I began to recover a little strength after my long illness, I made Wednesdays my days for Witch Walks. Wednesdays are sacred to the fairies and to Odin, god of shamans, and I would place myself in his care. In this way, I was led, one Autumn Equinox, to a sacred hill a couple of miles from my house, where the ancient druids once worked, and where there are many legends of apparitions, mysterious lights, and strange events. At the summit of the hill, its granite spine protrudes like an altar. As I collapsed there, having exhausted my small stock of energy and fully expecting never to get up again, I encountered the presiding *genius* of the hill, a spirit I call the Old Man.

The hill opened, and he seized me in his arms and took me deep inside the hill, where I met some of its denizens and learned a few of its many secrets, before the Old Man returned me to the surface. But the experience was far from over, and to recover I sat beneath a circle of haw-thorns, laden with red fruit, on the side of the hill. The dryads of the trees emerged, exquisite ladies dressed in white and red, and crowned with chaplets of leaves and scarlet berries. They led me in a merry dance, and I un-derstood that the spirit of the hill changed from moment to moment, with the seasons and the passing of the days, that it was made from everything that lived on it, which at that instant, included me. The tree spirits gave me haw-thorn leaves to eat, and explained that if I ate something from the hill, the spirit of the hill would be lodged in my growing cells, and the place would always be part of me. As I left the hill, I felt full of energy and hope, and it was then that my real healing began.

I have had many Witch Walks, not all as intense as the one previously described, but all life enhancing and infor-mative experiences that can only be gained with a mind and heart open to the power of the Otherworld.

Hallowing the Eyes

The 12th-century historian Saxo described how one must first hallow the eyes before being able to see spirits and to be safe in their presence. There are numerous ac-counts of the eyes being prepared in special ways in order to see the fairies.

It is said that a special ointment is applied to the eyes of newborn fairy babies to enable them to see the invis-ible. In some cases human midwives are called upon to perform this task, and occasionally these women have ac-cidentally got some of the ointment in their own eyes and afterwards been able to see the fairies coming and going.

One of the earliest tales, related in *Otia Imperialia* by Gervase of Tilbury (13th century C.E.), concerns the serving maid Eilian of Garth Dorwen who ran off with the Twyleth Teg (the Welsh "Fair Folk"). Nine months later her old mistress, the midwife of Llandwrog, was summoned to a birth. She was taken to a large cave in which there was a magnificent room with a woman on a fine bed. After the birth the husband asked the midwife to anoint the baby's eyes with magick ointment. As she did so her own eye began to itch and she rubbed it, accidentally getting some of the salve into it. Instantly she saw that the cave was really small and mean, and that the wife was on a bundle of rushes and withered ferns. She recognized Eilian, her old servant. Some weeks later she encountered the fairy husband in the market place at Caernarfon and asked how Eilian was getting on. He inquired which of her eyes she could see him with. When she told him he put it out with a bulrush.

A similar story was told in Germany. A midwife was taken to a hidden chamber and attended the birth of an elf. The fairies kept her with them for a few days, but she noticed that each time they went out they rubbed their eyes with a salve that they kept in a glass jar by the door. She smeared a little on her right eye. Eventually the woman was allowed to leave, and given as her reward the sweepings behind the door. She arrived home and her husband was overjoyed to see her again. Then she emptied her apron onto the table and the sweepings had turned into a big pile of gold. Some time later she attended a market in Frankenberg and saw a number of elves in the crowd, playing tricks and stealing from the stalls. They were invisible to everyone else. She called out to them and they inquired which eye she could see them with. When she told them her right, she instantly went blind in that eye and never saw through it again.

These are warning tales about what happens to the merely curious. Only the committed witch or shaman who acts with respect may deal with fairies with impunity. In reality, it is the *Third Eye* that should be anointed with a specially prepared ointment or oil to open *the sight*. The Third Eye is an energy centre, or chakra, whose position corresponds to the centre of the forehead. It is this centre that deals with the psychic senses and enables sight of the Otherworld.

Moon and Sun Oil

At the first waxing of the moon, take 13 white rose petals and put them in a glass jar. Cover them with almond oil. Place the jar outside each night for three nights. Do not let the light of the sun touch it at any point. Pour off the oil into a clean jar, and bury the rose petals beneath an apple tree. Now put into the oil three hollyhock flowers, three marigold flowers, nine young leaves from a hazel, and nine sprigs of thyme. Put the jar in the sun for three days. Do not let the moonlight touch it at any point. Strain off the oil into a clean jar. Bury the herbs under an oak tree. Dab a little oil onto the Third Eye position in the centre of your forehead when meditating on the fairies or otherwise working with them.

Four-Leafed Clover (*Trifolium sp.*) Salve

A four-leafed clover allows you to see fairies and other spirits. A milkmaid accidentally picked a four-leafed clover with the grass she used to soften the weight of the pail on her head. When next she looked at her cow she saw dozens of fairies milking it. A salve of four-leafed clover will also open the Sight.

> 7 four-leafed clovers
>
> 2 Tbs. almond oil
>
> 1/2 oz. beeswax

Method: Place the oil and clovers in a small pan and heat gently for 15 minutes. Meanwhile, place the wax in a fireproof basin over a pan of boiling water until it melts. Remove from the heat. Pour in the oil and clovers, and beat until the mixture sets. Use to anoint the Third Eye.

Four-Leafed Clover Charm

> 1 four-leafed clover
>
> 7 grains of wheat
>
> 3-inch square of purple cloth
>
> 1 piece of white thread

Method: Lay the four-leafed clover and the seven grains of wheat on the cloth, and tie up the parcel with the white thread, knotting it seven times. Carry the charm with you when you wish to encounter fairies, but do not carry it continually. It will work on seven occasions.

Fern Seed Charm

At midnight on Midsummer Eve, go quietly to a place where ferns grow. Take the almost invisible seed from them. On Midsummer's Day, place the seeds and some almond oil in a pan and heat gently for 15 minutes. Allow the oil to cool and strain away the seeds. Bottle the resulting oil in a dark glass bottle. When you want to see fairies, use some of the oil to anoint the Third Eye and the eyelids.

Rosemary Libation

A libation is an offering to the spirits. Fairies are particularly fond of rosemary. Take 1/2 oz. rosemary leaves and pour 1/2 pint of boiling water over them. Stand for 15 minutes and strain, discarding the leaves. Take the rosemary infusion, and pour onto the ground at a fairy haunted spot saying:

> *Spirits of this place*
> *I give to you this offering of holy rosemary*
> *In true fellowship and all honour.*
> *As I give to you and pay tribute to you*
> *So may you know me as fairy friend*
> *And aid me in my work.*

Sounding the Basins

This ritual is performed on Midsummer Eve in Brittany to summon the fairies. Place seven silver coins and seven naturally holed stones in a copper basin. The basin is shaken, or sounded (*senin ar c'hirinou*).

Holed Stones

Naturally holed stones are considered magickal. Fairies can be seen through such stones, especially those rocks worn through by water, such as the one at St. Nectan's Glen in the county of Cornwall in Southwest England.

There was a lazy young girl who hated spinning and avoided it whenever she could. She was playing truant on one occasion when she found a self-holed stone near a stream. Peering through the cleft the girl was amazed to see into a fairy mound where a strange little woman sat spinning, pulling out the thread with a huge, long lip. She was none other than the fairy Habetrot. It was soon arranged that the fairy would spin her thread.

The mother was delighted with the smooth thread and ran back and forth boasting how her daughter had spun so well. A passing laird thought what a good wife the girl would make and married her, bragging of all the spinning she would do after the wedding. He presented his bride with a new spinning wheel and plenty of fresh flax.

The unhappy girl went down to the holed stone and called on Habetrot. The kindly fairy considered the problem and advised the girl to bring her husband to visit the fairy spinners. The couple was shown into the mound and the laird was horrified at the deformed backs and lips of the women.

"Yes, we were all bonnie once, until we took up the spinning," Habetrot said, "Yon girl will soon be the same after pulling out the thread with her sweet red lips and bending her lovely young back over the wheel!" The laird was horrified at the prospect of his pretty young bride losing her looks. He took his wife home and forbade her to do any spinning, passing it all on to the fairies instead. So all worked out well in the end.

Small naturally holed pebbles, called hag stones, were once collected as protective talismans, strung together and hung in the barn or house, or attached to the house key, a double protective measure of hag stone and iron.

—— POTIONS TO HELP YOU SEE FAIRIES ——

Some herbs and flowers have the ability to open the sight. Many of these are very dangerous, even deadly, and this is not the place to speak of them. Here are some very safe recipes that you can use to help you open the portals of perception a little. (Note: Some people have allergies to herbs. Please check with an herbal practitioner before using.)

Thyme Tea

2 tsp. dried thyme

1 cup boiling water

Method: Infuse together for 10 minutes. Strain and drink.

Violet Tea

1 tsp. violet flowers and leaves

1/2 cup boiling water

Method: Pour the water over the herb and infuse for 5 minutes. Strain and drink.

Clary Sage Tea

2 tsp. clary sage

1 cup boiling water

Method: Infuse for 15 minutes and strain, adding a little sugar or honey to taste. Clary sage is a herb of divination. It is traditionally used at Midsummer when the entrance to the Otherworld is sometimes visible in the owl light of dusk and dawn.

Flying Ointment

1 part dittany of Crete

1 part cinquefoil

1 part parsley

1 part mandrake root

1 part calamus

1 part valerian root

1 part catnip

1 part mugwort

1 part damiana

6 parts petroleum jelly

a few drops fennel oil

a few drops clary sage oil

Method: Heat the petroleum jelly in a double boiler. Add the herbs and heat until the fat has extracted the scent, which will take about 30 minutes. Strain through cheesecloth into glass jars, and add a few drops of fennel and clary sage oil to each. Go to a fairy haunted place at midnight and anoint your whole body with the flying ointment.

Strawberry Wine

5 lbs. strawberries

2.5 lbs. sugar

juice and grated peel of 1 lemon

yeast and nutrient

1 cup of strong black tea

Method: Remove the stalks from the strawberries and wash. Place in a fermentation bin and add the peel and lemon juice, tea, and sugar. Add 6 pt. boiling water, allow to cool, and then stir in the yeast and nutrient. Cover and leave for a week, stirring daily. Strain into a demijohn, top up with cooled, boiled water, and fit an airlock. More sugar can be added for a sweeter wine. When fermentation is complete rack into a clean demijohn and leave to clear. When clear, bottle in dark glass bottles to preserve the colour. Take a glass of strawberry wine to help you open the sight during rituals and spells connected with the wildfolk.

INCENSES TO ATTRACT FAIRIES

Blodeuwedd Incense

1 part broom flowers

1 part bean flowers

1 part horse chestnut flowers

1 part oak flowers

1 part meadowsweet flowers

1 part flowering nettle

1 part primrose flowers

1 part hawthorn flowers

1 part flowering burdock

1 part blackthorn flowers

1 part corn cockle flowers

Method: Blend together and burn on charcoal blocks. Blodeuwedd is a Welsh fairy goddess, made of nine types of flowers.

Fairy Attraction

1 part violet flowers
1 part rosemary leaves
1 part rose petals
1 part lavender flowers
1 part bluebell flowers
3 parts oak bark
3 parts frankincense
1 part acacia
few drops lavender oil

Method: Blend together and burn on charcoal.
Use when meditating on fairy contact.

Rosemary Incense

The fairy folk are also particularly fond of rosemary
and the incense attracts them. Simply burn a few dried
rosemary leaves on charcoal.

FAIRY RITUALS

Elf Blot Ritual

The old Anglo-Saxons left offerings, called *blots*,
of meat and milk on the ancient burial mounds for the
elves. They did this to solicit healing, to ask for plentiful harvests. In Sweden, *alfablots* ("sacrifices to the
elves") were large community festivities to honour the
elves and ask them for good harvests.

Go to a fairy mound at twilight, taking with you some unpasteurized milk and fresh bread that you have baked yourself. Lay the bread on the mound and pour the milk around it, saying:

> *People of the Otherworld*
> *I bring you this sacrifice*
> *Wholesome bread and the whitest milk*
> *In return grant me your blessings.*
> [State then what you need.]

Elf Friend Ceremony

Prepare a garland of lavender flowers, rosemary, violets, and fern leaves, all of which you must pick yourself. Prepare also an incense of fairy attraction, of which you must have picked and dried all the flowers yourself, which are then added to the resins, which may be purchased. Go to a fairy haunted place at dawn, taking with you a bottle of homemade blackberry wine, a cup, and some cakes you have made yourself, the incense, some charcoal blocks with a fireproof dish to put them on, and your garland.

Light the incense and put on the garland. Say:

> *Spirits of this place I call to you. Spirits of*
> *this place I honour you. Attend me now and*
> *witness my intentions.*

Pour some of the wine into the cup. Pour a few drops on the ground, saying:

> *Spirits of this place, I make this offering to you.*

Drink some of the wine.

Take the cakes, and crumble one onto the ground, saying:

> *Spirits of this place, I make this offering to you.*

Eat one of the cakes.

> *Spirits of this place draw near and listen to my words. I come to honour you, to pledge to you that I shall honour the sacred Earth on which we both live; I shall not pollute or harm it. I shall honour the wild places and hold sacred the creatures of the Earth, my brothers and sisters of fur and fin, of leaf and bark. I shall hold sacred the cycles of the seasons and be part of the dance of the Earth.*

> *Like you, spirits of this place, I shall be brave and compassionate, humble and honourable, taking no more than I need, and treading softly on the Earth. I shall be wild, I shall be free.*

> *Test my words, and if you find them truthful, spoken from my heart, then accept me as your friend. If you find them false then treat me accordingly.*

Sit quietly for a while and listen to the world around you. You may see evidence of spirit presence, or hear voices in the trees, whispering in the wind.

When you are ready to leave, get up and leave the rest of the cakes, pour the wine onto the ground, and say:

> *Spirits of this place, you have listened to*
> *my words and weighed my intentions. I go now,*
> *but I shall hold you in my heart. Spirits of this*
> *place, hail and farewell.*

It is important to build up a relationship with the place that you work, and the spirits that inhabit it, over a period of time. It would be foolish to descend on a spot and demand its energies; it takes a long time for the spirits to get to know you and trust you. You should carry out most of your magickal work in the same place. Over the years, it will become more and more powerful, and you will gain the trust of its spirits.

4
Spirits of the Year

here are certain seasons, days, and hours that see fairies at their most active, times when they are more likely to be encountered by human beings. These are the critical points of balance in the day, week, month, or year, with dawn and dusk at the rising and setting of the sun, noon, midnight, and the first and second halves of the month. Both Celts and Anglo-Saxons believed that there were three spirit nights in the year, when creatures such as the fairies were abroad, when the veils between the worlds were thin. These nights were May Eve, Halloween, and Midsummer Eve.

For the ancient Celts there were only two seasons: summer, which began at Beltane (May 1st), and winter, which began at Samhain (November 1st). Western European fairies also observe this division of the year. Good fairies are most active from Beltane to Samhain and bad fairies from Samhain to Beltane. At Beltane, the winter fairies, represented by various Hags and unhallowed creatures, give up their dominion over the land. Good fairies are most active from Beltane to Samhain echoing the ancient return of the gods of summer and increase. Samhain marked the start of winter, and the ancient Celts celebrated it as a Festival of the Dead. Good fairies such as the Irish

Tuatha Dé Danaan and the English Puck retire from sight until spring returns. Evil fairies, such as the Scottish Unseelie Court, become very active; goblins are seen consorting with ghosts and evil omens such as Black Dogs, and Washer at the Ford manifest.

The greatest fairy festival is Midsummer, the ancient celebration of the Summer Solstice. At this time they are said to have their utmost power and be at their most frolicsome, whirling round the midsummer bonfires in an attempt to extinguish them.

Herbs collected on the fairy days have great power for healing, divination, and magick. They should be gathered, taken home and dried on these occasions.

IMBOLC (2nd FEBRUARY)

On this day, the winter hag fairy transforms into the maiden of spring. Imbolc was an old Celtic festival that marked the first stirrings of spring and was Christianised as Candlemas.

THE VERNAL EQUINOX (21st MARCH)

At the Spring Equinox, as the weather starts to brighten and the earth blossoms a number of fairies start to become busy. Scandinavian fairies are at their most active at this time, and if they are denied their rightful portion of the Equinox feast you will have to give them twice as much at Midsummer or you will be troubled until the next spring. The Russian cellar fairies, the *Domoviyr*, shed their skins and grow lighter ones for the summer.

MAY EVE

The Celts called the May Eve festival Beltane, and it stood between winter and the start of summer—a critical point of balance in the year. All fairies hold great festivals at Beltane and try to steal the ritual fire and the fresh butter made by humans. The Lunatishee, Irish blackthorn Fairies, guard the sacred thorn and will not allow it to be cut on May 11th (Old Beltane). Every seventh year on May Eve fairies fight for the rights to the harvest, for the best ears of grain belong to them. Fairies are particularly active on this day and sometimes may be glimpsed about their business. Anyone sleeping beneath a hawthorn on May Day is liable to be kidnapped by fairies.

Every May Day, King Gwyn ap Nudd and Gwythr, son of Greidawl, fight for the hand of the fairy maiden Creiddyledd. According to the story she married Gwythr but was abducted by Gwyn ap Nudd before the marriage could be consummated. King Arthur was appealed to, and he decreed that the two men should fight for her hand every May Day until Judgement Day. This is a seasonal battle between the powers of winter and summer for the hand of the Earth Goddess.

A number of fairies become active around this time, particularly those associated with vegetation, the spring and summer, and forests spirits such as Puck and Robin Goodfellow. In England, May Day was called Robin Hood's Day and was celebrated with morris dancing, circling the maypole, and gathering hawthorn blossoms from the greenwood. Robin Hood may have been a forest spirit in the manner of his namesake, Robin Goodfellow.

---------------- WHITSUNTIDE ----------------

The Russian river fairies, the *Rusalki*, make their first appearance of the year on Holy Thursday. In the sixth week after Easter, they move into the trees. In the seventh week after Easter, these water nymphs gather feathers and straw to make underwater nests. During this time humans are forbidden to sew, spin, or do any fieldwork. Their special time, however, is at Whitsuntide, when they are most vigorous, bathing in lakes and rivers or sitting on the shore combing their hair in the moonlight, asking women for dresses and girls for a skirt. At that season women hang strips of cloth torn from their dresses on the branches of birch trees to propitiate them. The fairies weave cloth and wash it in the stream, leaving it on the bank to dry. At Whitsuntide people stay indoors at night and do not bathe in the streams and rivers, clap their hands or do any field work that might offend the nymphs. Only witches dare swim in the water with the Rusalki.

---------------- MIDSUMMER ----------------

The best time to see fairies is on Midsummer Eve. Midsummer is the most ancient of festivals, derived from Pagan celebrations of the Summer Solstice, but Christianized as St. John's Day. It is one of the most mystical times of the year, when all sorts of bewitchments are in the air. Wreaths of eerie mist often surround mounds, fairy rings, stone circles, and other magickal places. Should you find a gap in the mist you will be able to pass through into the Otherworld.

On this night the fairy mounds open and they may be seen feasting inside. Sometimes a procession of lights can be seen moving from one hill to another, and this is the fairies moving house or visiting their neighbours. They use well-trodden paths running in straight lines between the mounds.

On this night, fairies visit certain enchanted places, such as the Rollright Stones in Oxfordshire (England), where they pop out of a hole near the King Stone and dance around the circle. The mischievous fairy variously called Robin Goodfellow, Jack Robinson, or Puck plays tricks on the unwary who dare to venture out on Midsummer's Eve. He is believed to light the Midsummer bonfires himself.

In Ireland, fairies move amongst humankind, playing tricks which range from innocent pranks to inflicting death. It is at this time that they most often steal away human women to become their brides.[1] Midsummer is the particular festival of the fairy Aine, who lives in the mound called Cnoc Aine.

In the Shetlands the Selkies, who normally have the appearance of grey seals, shed their skins to become human on this night and dance upon the seashore. Also, the Trows perform a lop sided crouching and hopping dance called *Henking* at Midsummer, which is one of their great festivals

In Russia, the Rusalki walk the land at Midsummer, and where they walk flowers appear. They are associated with fertility and when they move through the grain it causes it to grow.

LUGHNASA (2nd AUGUST)

This is another of the important fairy festivals, marking the start of the grain harvest. Several fairies become active at this time, such as the German Kornbocke, who causes grain to ripen, and the Russian Polevik, who kicks awake sleepy harvesters. In Britain and Ireland fairies hold processions or move house at Lughnasa, and sometimes a line of lights can be seen moving from one hill to another.

Lughnasa was an ancient Celtic festival marking the start of the harvest at the beginning of August. It is named after the Irish god Lugh, a king of the Tuatha Dé Danaan. Lughnasa is still celebrated by the Anglican Church as Lammas ("Loaf Mass").

HALLOWEEN (31st OCTOBER)

Samhain was an ancient Celtic festival, known in modern times as Halloween, marking the start of winter and the ascendance of the powers of blight, decay, and death. It was the boundary between one year and the next, and so doubly magickal. At Samhain the material and spiritual world unite. After Samhain, ghosts, spirits, and evil fairies walk the land. Good fairies, such as the Irish Tuatha Dé Danaan and the English Puck, retire from sight until spring returns. Wicked fairies, such as the Scottish Unseelie Court, become very active from now until Easter. Evil omens, such as black dogs and the Bean-Nighe or Washer at the Ford, also appear.

After Samhain all the crops left unharvested belong to the fairies. In Ireland, Halloween is called Phooka Night and after this time he renders all the crops unfit to eat and spoils all the blackberries. Welsh gryphons blight any crops left in the field after Halloween and the Lunatishee will not allow Blackthorn to be cut on November 11th (Old Samhain before calendar changes).

In Scotland, the Cailleach Bheur ("Blue Hag") strides across the land, beating down the vegetation with her staff and hardening the earth with frost. When her season has fully set in, she brings the snow. As spring approaches, her power begins to wane, until at Beltane (May Day) she gives up her struggle, flinging her staff under a holly tree, and this is why no grass can grow there. She then shrinks to a grey stone to wait until her season comes again. It is said that if anyone can find her staff he or she will have the power of destiny over the human race.

She is a folk survival of a winter crone goddess, re-born each Samhain, the start of winter, and proceeds to blight the Earth with snow and cold. She has two sons, one black and the other white. Each year one of them will steal her single eye and chase her north, before marrying the Summer Maid.

She is one of a number of hag or crone fairies. Another is the Polish Marzanna, who is the personification of winter, a hag of death. Every spring, an effigy of Marzanna, together with her broom, was "drowned" to symbolize the end of winter and return of spring.

— MIDWINTER SOLSTICE (21ST DECEMBER) —

The Norse and Germanic people called this *Yule*. It is the longest night of the year, when the ancients believed that the powers of darkness held sway. Fires were lit as a form of sympathetic magick to encourage the "rebirth" of the sun. In Norse tradition, this was a festival of the dead, with ghosts being free to wander during the long hours of darkness. Some of the more unpleasant fairies increase their activity around this time. In the Orkneys, the Trows leave the Underworld and dance. In England, the Wild Hunt rides out, led by Herne the Hunter.

At Yule a wide variety of gift-giving fairies appear including Father Christmas, or Santa Claus. It is possible that he devolved from the Scandinavian/Germanic god Odin or Woden, who rode the skies at Yule wearing a red, bloody, flayed animal skin, punishing the wicked and rewarding the good. Perhaps the figure may be older still, originating in the druidic midwinter festivities and the Roman Saturnalia. In England, he is Father Christmas, in Germany Kris Kringle or Pelze Nicol ("Furry Nicholas" from his fur costume), who is titled *Schrimmerlreiter,* "Rider of the White Horse," one of the titles of Odin.

The Icelandic Jubuk visits houses at Christmas. He is a horned fairy, and, if he is well fed, he will leave without causing any harm, but if not he will spill the beer in the cellar and make the stored grain rot.

The Norwegian Julenisse ("Yule Fairy") delivers Christmas gifts. He looks like a little old man in red clothes. Similarly, in Sweden the Jultomte delivers gifts on Christmas Eve and is rewarded with a special seasonal rice pudding.

Between Christmas Day and Twelfth Night the German Frau Holda rides about in a wagon. Berchte ("bright one") destroys any spinning left unfinished. The Greek Callicantzaroi fairies gather to celebrate the solstice, staring at the sun and vanishing on Twelfth Night. The Italian Befana delivers gifts at the Epiphany.

The Twelve Days of Yule, as the newborn sun struggles to grow to manhood, were considered to be a particularly dangerous time, existing as a time of chaos before normal life resumes after Twelfth Night (or the Epiphany). In many places the Twelve Days are considered unblessed or "unbaptized." They belong to the creatures of the Otherworld, particularly those associated with winter, death, and dissolution, who might appear as black dogs, human-headed chickens, whirlwinds, or fire. In the Balkans, the Twelve Days belong to those fairies that are the dead souls of unbaptized children or suicides, to werewolves, and to demons. The Twelve Days bring storms, hail, cold, and Death, who takes away the sick and frail.

NEW YEAR

Father Frost is the soul of winter in Russia. On New Year's Day, he and his daughter drive their reindeer sleigh through Russia, rewarding good children with presents.

The Mittwinterfrau ("Lady of Midwinter") is a Croatian hag fairy who leads a procession of dead souls between Christmas and Twelfth Night. Her followers either reward or punish people, according to their desserts.

Father Time is the spirit of the old year, portrayed as an old man clad in a long robe, carrying an hourglass and scythe. As the New Year strikes, he gives way to the New Year Child, who grows into a new Father Time as the year progresses. He may be associated with Saturn (or the Greek Cronos "time"), whose festival was celebrated at the Winter Solstice.

5
Devas and Dryads

Deva

airies are natural energies, primal expressions of the life force of the Cosmos. The closer you work with Nature the closer you become to the world of fairy. It is best to leave a small uncultivated area in the garden for the free ranging of the Nature Spirits. If you can make this private, it is a good place to mediate and contact them.

The fairies in your garden will be those of the earth, those associated with plants and trees. It is thought by many that these creatures, sometimes called Devas, help plants to grow. They are fairies that occupy a mystical realm between the physical and spiritual plane, and are therefore sometimes referred to as "The Middle Kingdom." Devas are ethereal creatures, with bodies made of the very finest matter that seem to shine with an inner light. The energy that flows through them sometimes appears as flowing hair and wings, though they can take any form they wish. Their job is to give the world its material structure and especially to show plants how to grow and what form to take. Every plant, flower, or vegetable has its own Deva.

There is an English tale of an old woman who had a cottage with a pretty garden in which she grew tulips. The fairies loved to visit it and sang their babies to sleep in its shade. Their songs were sometimes heard in the wind, and it seemed that the flowers themselves were singing. Because the fairies paid them so much attention, the tulips remained in bloom all summer long. The old woman appreciated this and would never let a single flower be picked. In time, she died, and the new owner of the cottage rooted out all the flowers and planted herbs. The fairies were so upset that they cursed the garden, and it would grow nothing but weeds. But they remembered their old friend and tended her grave, which sprouted wonderful flowers that no human hand had ever planted.[1]

There are a wide range flowers that are particularly associated with fairies in one way or another. The following is a list of some of these plants.

FAIRY PLANTS

Bluebell

A bluebell wood is a place of fairy spells and enchantments. Witches often grow bluebells to attract fairies, and at one time their presence in a garden was a damning piece of evidence in a witch trial. In Somerset, in the south of England, it is believed that you should never go into the woods to pick bluebells, as it will anger the fairies. If you are a child you will never be seen again, as the fairies will take you away, but if you are an adult, you will be pixy-led and will not be able to find your way out of the woods until someone rescues you.

Cowslips (*Primula veris*)

These lovely spring flowers are cherished and protected by the fairies. Cowslips are sometimes called Lady's Bunch of Keys or Culver's Keys, and unlock the doors to the fairy mounds of the English West Country and the treasure beneath them.

Fairy Ring Mushrooms (*Marasmius oreades*)

These rings of mushrooms, which appear on lawns and in meadows, leaving a circular bare patch, are a favourite dancing place of the fairies.

Fly Agaric (*Amanita muscaria*)

This red and white spotted mushroom is closely associated with fairies: perhaps that is why they wear red caps. The mushroom causes hallucinations and was used by witches and shamans to produce visions and to travel to the spirit worlds. The ancient Celts, among others, had a taboo on eating red food, which was believed to belong to the spirits or to the ghosts of the dead. (**Note:** These mushrooms are *deadly* poisonous.)

Four-Leafed Clover (*Trifolium sp.*)

The four-leafed clover enables the possessor to see fairies and spirits, to heal illness, and to gain good fortune. Four-leafed clovers will dispel any unwanted fairy magick.

Foxglove (Digitalis purpurea)

The common name "foxglove" may be a corruption of "folksglove," the glove of the Good Folk or fairies who, like the flowers, inhabit the woody dells. This has given rise to many of the plant's folk names: Fairy's Glove, Fairy's Cap, Fairy's Thimbles, Fairy Petticoats, Fairy Weed, Little Folk's Gloves, and Goblin's Thimbles. Grow foxglove in your garden to attract fairies.

Heather (Calluna vulgaris)

Fairies are said to feed on the stalks of heather. It is an ingredient of many recipes dating from around 1600, that allowed one to see fairies.

Primrose (Primula vulgaris)

In Celtic lore, the primrose is a fairy flower. It can make the invisible visible, and to eat primroses is a sure way to see fairies. If you touch a fairy rock with the right number of primroses in a posy (probably 13) it will open to Fairyland and fairy gifts, but the wrong number opens the door to doom. In Somerset, 13 primroses were laid under baby's cradle to protect it from being taken by fairies. In Buckinghamshire on May Eve, primrose balls were hung over the house and cowshed door to protect the beasts from fairies.

Ragwort (Senecio jacobaea)

Fairies sometimes bury their treasures beneath ragwort stalks, and these weeds are used as horses by fairies when they want to fly. The magick words to make them work are "Horse and Hattock!" One Cornish man rode a ragwort to Fairyland and back again.

Reed (*Phragmites communis*)

In Gaelic, the reed is called "the Distaff of the Fairy Woman" (*cuigeal nam ban sith*). The Gaelic word "*gaothaiche*" also relates to the reed and means "hollow." It refers to the mouth of the bagpipe. The pipes were originally made from reeds and in Celtic legend the fairies invented the bagpipe. Because of its thick root the Celts identified the reed with a submerged dryad.

Silverweed (*Potentilla anserine*)

This weed is turned up by the plough in spring. One of its old names was "seventh bread." It is said that fairies like to eat it, and it is probably assigned to them because it grows underground.

Toadstools

Mushrooms and fungi, with their unearthly shapes and rapid growth, are often associated with fairies, as evidenced by some of their names, which include Yellow Fairy Club, Slender Elf Cap, Dune Pixie-Hood, and Dryad's Saddle.

Wild Thyme (*Thymus vulgaris*)

At midnight on Midsummer's Night the King of the Fairies dances with his followers on thyme beds. In Shakespeare's *A Midsummer Night's Dream*, Oberon tells Puck, "*I know a bank where the wild thyme blows/ Where oxlips and the nodding violet grows.*" One charm states that to see fairies you should make a brew of wild thyme tops gathered near the side of a fairy hill and grass from a fairy throne. Like other fairy flowers, wild thyme is unlucky to bring into the home.

Lavender

Helping to calm the body and the mind, lavender helps to achieve the state of stillness you need in order to be able to see fairies.

Violet

Violets are associated with the twilight, a magickal "time between times," when the Otherworld is closer and is easier to slip into. Violet wine or tea may be taken at twilight to facilitate passage into the Other Realms. Violet wine may be used as the ritual drink on the eve of summer or Winter Solstice, whilst watching the sun rise or go down.

COMMUNICATING WITH THE SPIRIT OF YOUR GARDEN

Every garden, no matter how small, has a guardian spirit of its own, a *genius locus*. To speak to the protective spirit, choose a quiet place in the garden, and open your heart to it. Speak quietly, and ask for its help to make the most of your garden as a place of beauty that humans and fairies can share. When you are planning changes in the garden, when you are planting, weeding, and pruning, ask it to oversee the work.

Deva Contact When You Don't Have a Garden

Keep something living and green within your home to represent the world of nature and bring a living Deva into your home in the form of a house plant.

———————— TREE SPIRITS ————————

The most usual place to find fairies is in the forest. In its depths, the traveller encounters the lovely White Lady by the fountain, the elves in the clearings, the delicate Moss Maidens, roaming Centaurs and Sileni, and wild men and women lurking in the undergrowth. Fairies are closely connected to trees, either living in hollow trees or clearings, or manifesting as the spirits of the trees themselves.

In Greek myth, Dryads are tree nymphs living in secluded trees, far away from the prying eyes of men. Each has her own sapling and can merge with it at will, so that the chance passerby will only see a slender, graceful tree. She has a very special relationship with it, and if it is cut down, she will die in the same instant. Nevertheless, on the night of the full moon, all the dryads leave their homes to dance together through the moonlit glades of the forest.

In England, similar fairies were called Green Ladies. They dwell in oak, elm, apple, willow, holly, and yew trees. People honoured the Green Ladies by placing primroses beneath their trees.

In the forests of Germany, fairies called Moss Maidens spin the moss for the forests. They live in groups, and are grey and covered in moss themselves, in order to blend

Dryad

in with the trees. Their faces are old and withered. They get angry at humans who peel bark from trees, but generally, they help people they like, knowing the curative powers of all the forest plants. All forest fairies know about the powers of herbs, and it is from them that witches learn their herb craft.

Much of the world's landmass was once covered in forest. Trees were widely venerated among early people and believed to embody the spirit of a god or goddess, or that of a vegetation or nature spirit. Trees were also oracles, with spirits speaking through the whispering of the leaves. One of the oldest shrines of ancient Greece was the oak grove at Dodona, where the trees were believed to give prophetic utterances. The seers who interpreted the prophecies, called the Selli, received their oracle by listening to the clinking of bronze vessels hung in the trees, the calling of doves and other birds, the rustling of the oak leaves, or directly from the oak itself when they placed their heads on its heart.

The ancient Druids worshipped their gods in sacred groves called *nemetona*, which were restricted to the priesthood. The Germanic peoples also worshipped their spirits in forest clearings, and distrusted temples of bricks and stone. Many cultures have held trees to be sacred to the spirits that inhabited them. Even today, people instinctively feel that a tree has a spirit or consciousness. We sit with our backs to trees that we feel comfortable with and are comforted by them.

Trees are rooted in the earth with their branches in the heavens; they represent the union of the two brought into the middle world, our own physical plane. It is for

this reason that many sages are said to have reached en-
lightenment under sacred trees. Trees live for a long time,
are intimately connected to the Earth, experience much,
and become wise in their own way.

We still honour the spirit of the tree when we decorate the evergreen Christmas tree and place the fairy, which
represents its living spirit, at the top.

Taking a Wand

When you take a branch for a wand or other magickal
purpose, it should be taken from the living tree, and in
this way it is connected to the spirit of the tree. It has
more potency than anything you could ever buy, no matter how elaborate or expensive. A dead stick from the
forest floor has no power. A branch taken by force will
always act against you.

Sometimes, on a Witch Walk, you will be taken to a
place where the tree spirits are willing to contact you or
give you something. When you find such a place, you
may feel the tug, you may feel unease or a tingling on
the back of the neck or in the solar plexus (pit of the
stomach).

When you take something from a tree or plant,
always leave something in return, something that has value
to you, whether it is a bracelet or a silver coin. It should
be something that is a wrench to part with, not something of no value to you. Consider what it costs the plant
to give you your gift, and make a reciprocal return. You
might help a tree by tidying the area, planting new native
trees where there are few, and so on.

Your wand will always be connected to the spirits of the place and of the tree you took it from. This was the experience of Ron Fox, one of my students:

While at a gathering to celebrate Lughnasa one year, I sat reading through the coming ritual, quietly taking in the peacefulness of the fields and woods that surrounded me. I watched two field thrushes fly in across the field and land near some bushes; they walked in, out, and around the bushes near to one of the entrances to the woods. My intuition told me this seemed unusual and out of the ordinary. I'd not been told where the ritual was to be held, so that evening when everyone started to gather at one of the entrances to the wood, the same place the two birds had landed and performed their dance to make their presence known (to all that were taking notice), it once more stirred my instinct. To my surprise it turned out to be the same place in the wood I had been drawn to visit earlier that afternoon. In this small area, encircled by holly bushes with only one entrance in and out, the rite took place.

The next morning, I was, once again, sitting on my camping chair enjoying my first cup of tea. Again two field thrushes flew in from the same direction across the field and landed at the entrance to where we had held the rite the night before, again running in and out of the bushes and around the entrance to the wood.

Later, Anna sat next to me and we started talking of perception, the web, what she was seeing, feeling, and experiencing at that moment. It wasn't long before we were concentrating on the moment and all that was around us, tuning out the everyday chatter and concentrating our minds and senses to a point of alertness to try and perceive more than the physical. We entered the woods, again at the entrance near where the birds had been dancing. Without my foreknowledge, we ended up in the circle surrounded with holly bushes that we had been in the night before. I started to feel a little emotional and decided to let these feelings surface and let the meditation take its own course. My meditation deepened to the point where I lost my awareness of the physical place I was in, along with the people that were there with me.

I found myself in the wood on my own, feeling uneasy and knowing I was not alone. I came across a grey figure surrounded with bright light and knew instinctively what I had to do; I ran over and embraced it. As this happened I felt elated, the pain, anguish, and suffering I had experienced in my life were taken from me and drained into the earth where we stood.

The next thing I knew I was back, aware of the place and people I had been with inside the circle of holly bushes. I knew I had been touched by something beyond any physical experience I knew of, or could remember, that this had been a wonderful gift given to me by something outside of our everyday physical reality.

It did not end here. As the rest of the group came to the end of there guided pathworking, I was still feeling very out of sorts and emotional, so I left the group to have a few moments to myself. I walked into the woods and began to sit down next to a stream that runs through it. As I was about to sit, I saw a single holly leaf on the ground. Again I felt overwhelmed and emotional; jumping to my feet I stood astride two large boulders that were in the centre of the stream. I felt as if I was going to be sick, but as I leaned forward I was aware of myself repeatedly belching out what looked like dark particles onto the surface of the water. Again, I knew this was the harm and hurtful things I had suffered in my past being expelled from my body. When this was over I had the knowledge that I had been given a clean sheet, so to speak, a spiritual cleansing of the past harm I had suffered. This had been a very strong contact with the Otherworld and my high-sense perception; it was unnerving to say the least.

I spoke of what had happened with Anna, and she was surprised I had not taken a holly wand for myself that weekend, but I knew that weekend's experience had not been about the gaining of a wand. Four weeks later, odd things were happening at home and around me, not all good, almost as if I were being tested. I found myself able to deal with all this adversity in a more calm and understanding way than I had been able to before my encounters with the spirit in the woods.

Weeks after this, Anna and I were gathering firewood for an upcoming festival. As we talked, I started to feel the unease I had felt in the woods in Wessex. Anna suggested that I was being called. I went further into the woods alone and once more, after a few minutes, I was somewhere else: the Otherworld. I cannot remember much of what happened on this occasion, but came back to wakefulness when a large raindrop falling from high in a tree hit me on the ear. I must have been there a while because I struggled to stand, my legs were really stiff and aching because of the way I had been leaning with my back against the tree.

As I tried to regain my senses, I became aware that I was standing next to a holly bush, one I recognized: It was one I had perceived to have a strong brightness about it on a previous visit to our wood. A strong voice in my mind told me to take a branch for a wand, almost shouting in urgency, "Take a wand! Take a wand!" This I did, but it was not easy and I almost stopped, feeling uneasy because I felt the pain the tree was feeling, "Take it! Take it!" shouted the voice.

It was done. I had gained my wand. I returned to find Anna, pleased as punch. Look at me, a grown man with a stick in his hand, I thought. But I knew this was special; I had won, and been given my wand. After letting my holly branch dry out for a few weeks, I removed the bark and sat down to carve it into a wand for myself. The hours passed, and I let the shape and grain of the wood dictate how the wand would turn out to be. I carved,

*and my mind became quiet, as I followed the grain
the shape of two birds' heads became apparent. I
carved and they became a part the handle.*

*I know what the spirit and energies of a holly
bush feels like now. I knew the birds had relevance
to that moment in time. I know I had been given
guidance and healing from spirit and the
Otherworld on these and other occasions. I was
able to find out these things, and much more, by
taking the chance to set aside my normal blind-
folded view of reality, what we are told only exists
in the real physical world; to be observant in many
ways, not only in the physical, but also in my perception of the less solid spiritual energies and
events we interact with in ritual and our daily lives.
We need to put in lots of practice and study to
learn the techniques that will help us become more
aware and able interact with the Otherworld.*

Sensing the Tree Spirit

To attune your consciousness with that of a dryad,
you will need to slow yourself down a great deal. Trees are
long-lived, slow growing compared to humans; their state
seems dreaming to us, and we seem like hurrying, busy
insects to them.

Spend time with your chosen tree spirit. Spend time in
its shade, sleep beneath its branches in the summer. Nurture it, care for it, form a loving relationship with it, and
you will receive love and wisdom in return.

Still your mind, centre yourself, and slowly approach
the tree, palms out facing towards it. You will become

aware of an energy field surrounding the tree. No two trees are the same; every tree will be different. Some are open and friendly; others closed and guarded and others down-right hostile. This will depend on the experience they have had of humans, and what they are picking up from you. In spring they are more expansive and bold; in autumn, contracting and inward looking.

You may find your own energy can be recharged by sitting within the tree's energy field, with your back to the tree. When you are sad, sit with your back to a tree, and feel the comfort flowing from the tree to you.

Tree Alignment

Imagine that you have roots, like the roots of a tree, coming from your feet and extending into the ground. Draw up earth energy from these roots and allow it to flow up your body like sap rising.

Imagine that you have branches like those of a willow tree coming from your head, sweeping down to touch the earth. Allow the energy to flow through them back into the earth, completing the circuit. Do not try to retain this energy.

Breathe in and the energy rises up; breath out and the energy flows back to the earth. Allow the energy to pass through you; you do not generate the energy you use—you are a channel for them.

Wassailing the Tree Spirits Ritual

In winter, the apple trees are wassailed to honour the Apple Tree Man, the spirit of the orchard. His tree is always the oldest in the orchard, or the one that bears the heaviest crop. He can grant a good harvest for the whole orchard, and other benefits besides. The last of the crop should be left on the ground for him, and his tree should be wassailed at Yule or Old Twelfth Night, 6th January, or Old Twelfth Night, 17th January.

It is best to use some cider made from his apples, and this is warmed over a fire of ash wood. It has pieces of toast floating in it. Everyone present drinks the health of the tree and takes a piece of toast. The rest of the toast is put into the branches of the tree for the birds, and the remaining cider is poured on the roots of the tree. Everyone should bow to the tree, and sometimes shots are fired over it to scare away evil spirits. This song is sung to it:

"Old apple tree, we wassail thee,
and hoping thou wilt bear

For the Lord doth know where we shall be,
till apples come another year

To bear well and bloom well, so merry let us be
Let every man take off his hat and shout to the
old apple tree,

'Old apple tree, we wassail thee,
and hoping thou wilt bear

Hat-fulls, cap-fulls, three-bushel bagfuls
And a little heap under the stairs'

Hip! Hip! Hooray!"

In some places, such as Henfield, West Sussex, in the east of England, the custom is called "apple howling," which might be derived from "apple yuleing." Here the spirit of the tree is woken up with the blowing of horns, thrashing the tree, and chants of:

"Stand fast root, bear well top,
God send us a good howling crop.
Every twig, apples big!
Every bough, apples now!"

FAIRY TREES

Alder (*Alnus glutinosa*)

The alder tree grows near water and is said to be under the protection of the water fairies. The alder yields three dyes: red from the bark, green from the flowers, and brown from the twigs. These dyes are taken to represent fire, water, and earth. The green dye is associated with fairies' clothes, too.

Apple (*Malus sp.*)

In European mythology, legendary fairy isles of apples are common, and always lie in the west, the place of the dying sun, from which it proceeds to enter the underworld, or Land of Youth, travelling through the realms of death in preparation for its rebirth at dawn. All Neolithic and Bronze Age paradises were orchards; "paradise" means "orchard." Eating a fairy apple confers eternal youth, immortality, or rebirth. However, gaining the fruit is fraught with danger. The tree is always guarded, usually by a snake or dragon. Once the fruit has been eaten, the hero can never return to being what he was before. The fairy queen warned Thomas the Rhymer about eating the apples in her garden. She said that to partake of the food of the dead is to know no return to the land of the living.

Ash

The oak, the ash, and the thorn are the three great fairy trees, and it is here that the wildfolk can most often be found. It is associated with the Wyrd Sisters, or Fates, and was Odin's path to the Otherworld as he hung nine days and nights from its branches.

Birch (*Betula alba*)

In some parts of England a birch was hung with red and white rags and leaned against stable doors at Beltane (May Day) to prevent horses being "hag-ridden"—that is, being taken out by fairies and ridden. In Russia, the forest spirits called Lieschi were considered to be always present in clumps of trees, particularly the tops of birch trees. In Somerset, a female spirit called "The One with the White Hand" flickers from birch copses, pale and gaunt as the trees, to ambush young men.

Blackberry (*Rubus fructicosus*)

A taboo on eating blackberries exists in Celtic countries. In Brittany and Cornwall, the reason given is that the blackberry belongs to the fairy folk. Blackberry wine and jam make suitable offerings to the wildfolk. Leave some on the ground near their haunts.

Blackthorn (*Prunus spinosa*)

November 11th is recognized in Ireland as the day of the blackthorn sprites, the Lunantishees. These Otherworldly beings guard the sacred blackthorn from any human foolhardy enough to profane the sacred tree by cutting the wood at this time.

Elder (*Sambucus nigra*)

In Denmark, the elder was known to be under the protection of Hulda, the Elder Mother, and, in England, the Elder Mother or Elder Queen. She lived at its roots and was the mother of the elves. Whoever wished to take a branch or cut the tree had to first ask her permission; otherwise grave misfortune would follow.

Elm (*Ulmus sp.*)

The elm is also called "elven" in England because it is considered to be the dwelling place of elves.

Hawthorn (*Crataegus monogyna*)

The hawthorn is a tree very much associated with fairies; their trysting places are under its shade. It is said that when the oak, ash, and thorn grow close together, it is a favourite haunt of the fey folk and those solitary hawthorns growing on hills or near wells are markers to the world of the fairies. Any human who sleeps beneath one, especially on May Eve, is in danger of being taken away by them. Fairies are very protective of hawthorns, and a blooming tree should never be trimmed as it angers them, and always the tree should be trimmed east to west.

Hazel

The hazel tree has many connections with fairies. A 15th-century recipe for summoning fairies involved burying hazel wands under a fairy hill. The tree was called *bile ratha* in Ireland, meaning "tree of the rath"—that is, a fairy fort. Boiling jam was stirred with a hazel or rowan stick to prevent the fairies from stealing it. Hazel is the commonest wood used to make a forked divining rod. In Britain, these were used for divining water and buried treasures, as well as guilty murderers. The divining rod was connected with elves and pixies who have all the treasures of the Earth in their keeping. It was traditionally cut on St. John's Eve, one of the notable fairy festivals. The fairies of English hazel thickets, who had names like Churnmilk Peg and Melch Dick, were said to inflict painful bloat and cramps on anyone who tore off unripe nuts, but they were probably angered more by the damage done to the trees than by the theft.

Oak (*Quercus robur*)

Fairies like to dance around old oak trees. Wood-wives (German forest fairies) frequent the old sacred forests and oak groves. Some tribes once worshipped a wood-wife between Christmas and Twelfth Night. Her clothes were kept in an old oak tree.

Elves live in oak trees and the holes found in the trunks are their means of entrance and exit. A New Forest (England) rhyme advises *"turn your cloaks for fairy folks are in old oaks"* (to turn your cloak inside out protects you from being distracted from your path by fairies).

In England unfriendly dwarfish creatures called Oakmen live in the saplings that grow from felled oaks. If bluebells are present, this is a sure sign of their presence. Oakmen may offer food to passing mortals that will turn out to be poisonous fungi disguised by magick.

Rowan (*Sorbus aucuparia*)

Rowan, or mountain ash, draws its name from the old Norse word *runa*, meaning "a charm." Some country folk call it "the witch tree" or the "wicken tree." The rowan is associated with protection, particularly from witchcraft, fairies, and lightning. When it grows in a garden, especially if it is self-seeded, it shows that the place is under the protection of the fairies.

—————— VEGETATION SPIRITS ——————

Early humans were hunter-gatherers, but during the Neolithic period became food-growers, dependant on the yearly cycle of planting, germination, growth, and harvest. In winter, the spirit of vegetation seems to die, to go down as seed into the underworld (where the fairies live) until it is resurrected the next spring.

Many nature spirits, or fairies as they may be called, are associated with vegetation, crops, and the fertility of the land, with the power of either blessing or blighting.

The Russian Polevik, or field fairies, grow with the grain and after the harvest shrink to the size of the stubble. A Polevik will retreat before the harvesters and hide in the last few stalks of grain. When these are cut he gets into the hands of the reapers and is taken to the barn with the final sheaf. If people wander into the fields at the wrong time, they disturb the fairies, who will cause them to cut themselves with the sickle. A Polevik may kick awake harvesters who have fallen asleep on the job. After late September, they claim any grain that has not been harvested.

The Polish equivalent is the Polewiki. (Pole means "field," hence the name of the country "Poland.") He appears as a dwarf with grass for hair and eyes of different colours, at noon or sunset, and will harm anyone that he finds asleep or drunk during the harvest period. Sometimes farmers in Poland pour the Polewiki libations and leave grain in the fields for them. The Polewiki rides about the fields on horseback and will trample down the sleepers or inflict illness on them. He strangles drunkards who trample the grain.

The Lusatian Serbs fear the Pripoldnica ("Midday Spirit"), who looks like a young woman carrying a sickle. She guards the growing corn from thieves and punishes anyone who treads the ears down.

Working With Plant Spirits

The old folk understood that there was a way of maintaining the natural balance, a way of harvesting, of keeping the life force of the plants. Plants are linked to the living Earth from which they spring, and the plant itself is always the teacher. Nature spirits were always contacted and consulted about growth and harvest.

Witches use plant powers, but to capture them without alienating or dissipating them is not simply a matter of walking three times around a tree and saying, "Can I have a branch," and leaving a coin in return. Trees and herbs are not really "used" magickally. When properly approached, they may share something of their life force, their spirit. Individual herbs and plants can be befriended as allies to enable the practitioner to travel to

Otherworldly places, and to become in tune with different energies.

Sometimes a plant or tree will call to you, and you should listen and trust your instincts. Every plant has a meaning, a place within the great pattern. Accept any insight that is given to you, no matter what the circumstances. If the herb is approached with love and trust, its force will harmonise with the witch and share its secrets. If the plant is taken with the wrong motives, if it is mistreated or misused, it may cause discomfort, mislead or seek to gain control of the witch. If an enemy is made of the plant spirit, it can destroy.

It is a common misconception that a plant needs to have hallucinogenic properties to facilitate expansion of consciousness. Only a small number of power plants are psychedelic, and these plant spirits are the most difficult to deal with. They easily overcome the weak will of anyone stupid enough to use them for recreational purposes. Every plant, from the common daisy to the mighty oak, has its own power and vibration, and by taking time to gain the trust of the plant spirit, these can be shared.

When working in conjunction with herbs and the wildfolk, the life force—or spirit—of the plant is more important than any "active ingredient"; you must begin by getting to know the plants that grow in your local area, those vegetation spirits that live with you, along your local hedgerow, meadow, park, or road, or in your garden. Get a good field guide to help you identify them and a reputable modern herbal to tell you what they may be used for. You will need to refer to the botanical name (usually Latin or Greek), because these names are specific, while the same common name can refer to several very different plants.

Spend time with the plants, noting where they live, in sun or shade, on chalky soil or sandy soil, and so on, their growth habits, when they flower, and when they set their seeds. Note the shape of the leaves, their texture, their colour, their taste, *if edible*. In this way you will begin to learn from the plants themselves. Each plant is a living teacher and must be approached as an individual spirit, a vital life force that may become your ally if approached with love and respect. It is a knowledge that cannot be bought and that cannot be learned from books, but only by doing. Allow yourself to trust your inner wisdom.

TAKING THE PLANTS

Each plant must be correctly approached and harvested in perfect condition. It must always be respected as a living being: its life force is the essence of its power.

Plant powers can be utilized in many ways, including the following:

(**Note:** Some herbs are poisonous, and some people have allergies to certain herbs. Please check with an herbal practitioner before use.)

Infusions

If the plant is edible (and please check this very, very carefully) you can eat it (you might nibble a few hawthorn or oak leaves, for example) or take it internally in the form of an infusion or decoction.

Hot Infusion (Teas or Tisanes)

Many of a herbs components, such as its minerals, vitamins, sugars, starches, hormones, tannins, volatile oils, and some alkaloids dissolve well in water, and for this reason, herbs are often taken as infusions or tisanes. Generally the difference between the two is simply of strength: An infusion is a medicinal dose, whereas a tea or tisane is weaker. Use 1 teaspoon of dried herb per cup of boiling water or 1 oz. per pint of boiling water. Pour the boiling water over the herb and infuse for five to 15 minutes.

Cold Infusion

Some herbs have properties that are destroyed by heat, so a cold infusion is made. Use a non-metal container and put in 1 oz. of the herb and 1 pint of cold water. Close the lid or cover with cling film and leave for five to six hours.

Decoction

Some seeds, roots, buds, and barks, and so on. need to be boiled in water for a while. This is called a decoction. If they are dried they should first be pounded into a pow-ered form. Use 1 oz. of dried herb or 2 oz. of fresh herb to 1 pint of water. Bring the mixture to the boil in a non-aluminium pan and simmer 10 to 15 minutes. Strain.

Shaman Smokes

Some plants have leaves that can be dried and smoked. Tobacco, for example, has a long history as a sacred plant. However, if you use a plant recreationally, if you are ad-dicted to it, you can never use it as a sacred herb. Other herbs that can be smoked include coltsfoot, peppermint, wild lettuce, passionflowers, broom flowers, and damiana.

Wands and Staffs

Woody plants can provide powerful magickal tools, such as wands and staffs. However, you will need to get to know the tree over a period of time; you will have to form a relationship with it, and ask for its permission. There will be a moment when the energies are right for taking the wood, and you must not miss it, or there may not be another chance. You should leave something in return, preferably something of yourself. When you have your wood, it must be left for a few months (depending on the type of wood) to season, then you can carve it of you wish. Do not varnish it, and do not add crystals until you have worked with the tool for a while, and intuit what would enhance its powers.

Talisman

Talismans can be made from herbs and flowers wrapped in cloth, and carried about the person, or wooden slivers carved with runes or suitable symbols.

Divination Tools

Rune and ogham sets can be made from wooden slivers and the power of the plant spirit invoked to help with the act of prophecy.

Incense

Incenses are made from dried flowers, herbs, leaves, roots, barks, seeds, resins, and wood. Each has its own property and will be much more powerful if you pick and dry these yourself with due reverence and ceremony. These are then combined and burned on charcoal discs (easily available from occult suppliers) or thrown on the bonfire.

Bathing Herbs

Tie bunches of fresh herbs beneath the hot bath tap as the water runs in to the bath. (**Note:** Do be sure to check that the herb is suitable for this purpose first.) Alternatively, tie a handful of dried herbs in a square of muslin, and drop this into the bath.

6
Fairy Families

We are used to stories of witches having familiar spirits. What is not generally realized is that these familiars were usually fairies, whether in the guise of humans, imps, or animals such as fairy cats or dogs. Familiars often shared the common names of the local fairies: Robin, Jack, Tom, Hob, Jill, Peg, and so on.

In 1646, John Winnick confessed that one Friday he was in his barn when a black shaggy spirit appeared to him, with paws like a bear, though it was smaller than a rabbit. The spirit asked him why he was so unhappy, and John replied that he had lost a sum of money, and the spirit agreed to help him. Stories of gaining a familiar often have similar, common elements—people in trouble or sick people are visited by a fairy who promises them a gift that is then faithfully delivered. The gift is usually one of knowledge—the power to cast spells, make herbal potions and cures, and so on—in other words, the power to become a witch.

A MacLeod called the Forester of the Fairy Corrie, who served with the Earl of Argyll's troops in 1644, had a *leannan sith* who followed him everywhere in the shape of a white fairy hind. Its presence irritated the earl and he ordered the forester to kill it. MacLeod told the earl that he would obey, though it meant his own death. As the shot hit the fairy, it gave a shriek and disappeared, while the forester fell down dead.

There is always a price to pay for possessing a fairy familiar. The Belvoir witch Margaret Flower, tried in 1619, said that she promised her familiars to fulfil their needs, in return for which they fulfilled her desires. The desires of fairies ranged from bowls of milk and offerings of bread, to human company, music, and even human blood.

Familiars were often said to drink the blood of their witches from specially formed "teats" on the witch's body. Ellen Shepherd, a Huntingdon witch, in 1646 said that she had four familiars in the shape of grey rats, which she fed with blood from her hips, and in return they granted her "all happiness." In 1582 Margery Sammon was given two familiars by her mother, two toads called Tom and Robin. Her mother advised her to feed them on milk; otherwise they would want to suck her blood.[1] The Irish always advocated leaving out water for fairies at night; otherwise they would be angry and suck sleepers' blood. In one story from Glen Rushen, on the Isle of Man, the fairies went onto a house one night to do some baking. The family had put no water out for them; they were heard to say, "We have no water, so we'll take blood out of the toe of the servant who forgot our water." From the girl's blood they mixed their dough and baked their cakes, eating most of them and poking the rest up under the thatch. The next day the servant-girl fell ill and remained ill until she was given a piece of the fairy cake that was hidden in the thatched roof.

On other occasions, familiars were simply fed with ordinary food. Margaret Moone fed her 12 imps with bread and beer. This has direct parallels with the feeding of a shaman's spirit allies in other cultures. In Malaysia, for example, a Bajang (a spirit/fairy) can be kept as a familiar by a magician who feeds it on eggs and milk.

This is reminiscent of the many stories of fairies being fed in return for their help. Bowls of fresh milk and cream were left by the hearth for brownies and other house fairies, such as the German Chimke. Before setting out on a journey, offerings of bread and milk were made to the Fridean, Scottish fairies that guard the roads. In Gotland, offerings of milk, beer, and flax seeds were made to the Disma fairies by being poured into a fairy ring.

—— HOUSE FAIRIES AND BROWNIES ——

Every house has its own spirit, which should be honoured in the proper way. In bygone Rome, this spirit was called the *Lar familiaris* ("household lar") and was given daily offerings of food and monthly gifts of garlands, all placed on the hearth shrine. Legends of similar house spirits are found throughout the world, from the Hawaiian Menahune to the British Brownie, the Spanish Duende, the German Hausmänner, the Russian Igosha, the Finnish Kodin-Haltia, and the North American Shvod and Cambodian Àràk.

The first thing that people did when they moved into a new house was to greet its resident spirit. For example, the Deduška ("Grandfather") is a Russian house fairy who appears as an old man covered in hair, often in the likeness of a family patriarch. He wears a red shirt, a cloak, and a red belt. He lives behind the oven or near the threshold of the house, in the cupboard, or in the stable, sometimes with his wife and children. He will protect the family, their home, and their livestock from bad luck, keep the servants in order, and do all kinds of chores about the place while everyone is sleeping. He is especially keen on spinning. To keep him happy he should be given something from each meal, and white linen should be placed in his favourite room. The family that pleases its fairy will prosper in all things but the family that fails to do him honour or uses bad language in his presence will suffer his anger. He will revenge himself on the crops and cattle or leave the house altogether. The unprotected family will then fall ill and die.

Brownies are solitary fairies found in Southern Scotland and the northern counties of England. They become attached to particular houses or families, and while the humans are asleep, they work about the house or farm, cleaning, tidying up, or help with the brewing. When the cock crows, it is to let the brownie know it is time to go to bed. The only reward they ask is a bowl of cream or best milk.

Brownies are fiercely loyal as long as they are well treated. A certain family had a brownie, and when the mistress was in labour, a servant was asked to go to Jedburgh for the midwife. The servant took his time, and seemed loath to go, so the brownie slipped into his coat and, taking the best horse, rode off towards town, taking the pregnant girl up behind him, much against her will. He rode heedlessly through the swollen River Tweed, riding with the speed of a spirit creature. Delivering the woman to the doctor's, he went home and up to the room of the slow servant, who was just putting his boots on. The angry brownie took up his whip and struck him several hearty blows. The master was so grateful that he had a new green coat made for the brownie, but this was a mistake. The brownie put it on and disappeared forever.

Brownies are very good at hiding and can make themselves disappear at will, but those who have seen them describe them as small, shaggy-haired, and ugly, with flat faces. They are often ragged in appearance, but they are offended by gifts of clothes and will promptly disappear forever if given a new suit, so if you have a helpful house fairy don't be tempted to reward it in this fashion. They are easily offended, and if they are mistreated they turn into destructive boggarts. House fairies often have a mischievous side and like to play tricks on the human inhabitants of a dwelling, particularly if they are not getting their due. Such pranks might include rattling the fire irons, smashing crockery, hiding objects, or just making a mess.

Spanish house fairies are called Duendes and look like small, middle-aged women with very long fingers, dressed in green, grey, or red; or old men wearing brimless, conical hats, dark hoods, or red caps. The fairies may move house with their human families. They come out at night, cleaning and repairing, but are sometimes so house proud that they act like poltergeists to get rid of the human beings that make the place a mess. They will pinch sleepers, breathe down their necks, touch them with icy fingers, or pull off the bedclothes.

House fairies often live in the hearth, or behind the stove. For the ancients, the hearth-place was the altar of the household gods, where offerings could be made. When you begin to think of your home as having indwelling spirit it can make a huge difference to the quality of life within it. You can use your mantelpiece as an altar, or you can make a small shrine or niche beside it. What you put on that altar is up to you. You might want a statue of a fairy to represent the house spirit.

MUSES

Surviving Celtic poetry tells us that poets found their inspiration by visiting the Otherworld. Celtic stories, both ancient and relatively modern, are full of visits to Fairyland. The bard Taliesin described a period spent in the Otherworld where he gained his poetic spirit. The story of the bard Thomas the Rhymer tells of his time in Fairyland, where he was given the apple of truth and initiation.

In Celtic lore, the nine hazel trees of poetic art grow about a stream or well in the Otherworld. There, poets drink and are thus inspired and refreshed. This may have some connection with the many magickal cauldrons that appear in Celtic myth. There seems to be some connection between fire and water in poetic inspiration. The nine muses blew upon the cauldron; each imparted a gift.

There are many clues that tell us that the Celtic bard was much more than a story-teller—that he was, in fact, akin to an initiated shaman who gained his knowledge and inspiration from the Otherworld. His poems express experiencing other realities, such as becoming various animals, he speaks of an initiatory drink, and there are descriptions of the provoking or experiencing of a shamanic crisis. He speaks with the spirits of the Otherworld (fairies and so on) and he mediated with, and interpreted, the spirits on behalf of others.

He used magick and made prophecies. The Irish word for bard, *fili*, meant "weaver of spells." The function of the poet was a magickal one. Like shamans in other countries, Irish poets wore feathered cloaks called *tugen*. Some say that these were of swan feathers; others describe them as multi-coloured or containing mallard feathers.

The bards carried wands or branches to denote their profession and status. It is thought that these had small bells on, which would be rung to call for silence when they were about to perform. The silver branch had another meaning; in several tales a silver branch is given to mortals by Queens of the Fairy, and it allows them to enter the Otherworld. Sometimes the branch has fruit and blossoms on one stem. Other branches had silver apples upon it, and these would ring to enable the poet to have a vision of the Otherworld; in Celtic myth the apple is the fruit of the Otherworld, the sustenance of its inhabitants and the food of the dead.

Some of the ancient poets and bards, such as the famed Carolan, learned their craft by sleeping on fairy hills and mounds, allowing the magickal music to enter their hearts and souls as they slept. Many old Irish tunes, such as "The Pretty Girl Milking the Cow" and "The Londonderry Air," are fairy songs.

In popular fairy lore, it is said that fairies can reward their favourites with the gift of music, poetic or artistic inspiration. These fairies may be called muses, a name that derives from the nymphs of inspiration in ancient Greek myth. They were invoked with willow wands and were the companions of Apollo. Their provinces were as follows:

Clio: memory and poetry (or history as we call it today)

Euterpe: flute playing

Thaleia: comedy

Melpomene: tragedy

Terpsichore: dancing and lyric poetry

Erato: love poetry

Polyhymnia: mime

Urania: astronomy

Calliope: epic poetry

In Celtic legend, the Leanan Sidhe is a muse who gives inspiration to her poet or musician lover. She sometimes takes the form of a woman to inspire men in battle with her songs. Those she favours have brilliant careers, but die young.[2]

In Welsh lore, Mab is queen of the Welsh fairies, the Ellyllon. In 16th- and 17th-century literature she was quean of the fairies, "quean" meaning muse or midwife from the Saxon *quen* "woman," though it was not babies she midwifed, but magick and dreams.

In modern Arabic lore, Shaitans are djinns, the children of the devil, but in pre-Islamic times, the Shaitans were very different. A Shaitan was a type of muse, or genius, inspiring poets and prophets.

If you put your ear to a fairy mound, you may be able to hear the unearthly strains of lovely music, plaintive and almost unbearably sweet. But be careful: Those who have heard the fairy music will never be the same again. One man who heard the fairy music was haunted by the melody day and night until he grew mad and had no pleasure in life. He longed to be with the fairies again and hear them sing.

—— FATES AND FAIRY GODMOTHERS ——

Fairy Godmothers appear at the birth of a child to predict its future or bestow gifts upon it. They are familiar figures throughout the Celtic, Germanic, and Slavonic cultures of Europe. They usually dress in white and appear three days after the birth of a child to bless or curse it, according to the behaviour of its family. They will foretell its future, give advice, and possibly favour the child with birthmarks. The house must be prepared for their arrival by being cleaned and thoroughly swept. The table must be laid with honey, bread, and three white almonds. In parts of Greece, water, coins, and gifts are placed beside the food. The door should be left open and a light should be left burning. The house should be kept quiet. Once the fairy has appeared and the fate told, it cannot be changed.

These fairies also appear at marriages, and girls who want the help of the Fairy Godmothers make pilgrimages to caves, leaving offerings of cakes and honey. The fairies are then invited to the resulting weddings, and honey-glazed almonds are distributed to the guests in their honour. The fairies appear once more at death, to take the soul out of the world.

We shouldn't forget that the word *fairy* comes from the Latin *Fatae*, or fate. These Fairy Godmothers are the ancient weaver goddesses who spin the life thread, measure it, and finally cut it. In Greek myth, they were the Moerae, in Rome the Fatae, and in Scandinavia the Norns. The 11th-century bishop of Worms rebuked women for their continued belief in the Parcae and for laying three places at meals for them. Chaucer and Shakespeare both mentioned three sisters of Fate. These original Fates controlled the destinies of humankind, bestowing gifts upon newborn children, measuring their adult lives, and finally ending them. They span the entirety of creation, a shimmering interweaving of filaments, viewed as a Cosmic net or web.

In the ancient world, the goddesses who created the cosmos with their spinning were also deities of magick. Magick is often spoken of as knotting or weaving, and magicians as spirit weavers, web weavers, or net weavers. In fact, the word *religion* comes from the Latin *religare,* meaning "to tie." Magick was performed by moving and weaving the threads of the cosmic net, or by knotting them. The Egyptian goddess Isis was the patroness of weaving but she also wove magick. The knot was one of her symbols, usually depicted as a knotted cloth between her breasts and represented in an amulet called a *tyet*. The Egyptians used knots for many magickal purposes, symbolising the controlling and releasing of both creative and destructive forces. In particular, seven knots were tied in a cloth to invoke the seven Hathors, of goddesses of childbirth, but Isis, Sekhmet, Amun, and Thoth were also invoked during rituals as knots were tied. The ancient Romans were so in fear of the power of the knot to bind and limit energies that the high priest, the *Flamen Dialis,* was forbidden to wear any knot or closed ring on his person, in case it bound up his powers. Similarly, Roman women who tied knots of twisted threads when they were passing crops were suspected of trying to "bind" the crop and cause its failure.

The cosmic threads weave in and out of this world and the Otherworld, because we are all part of the same cosmos. By following one of these threads it is possible to pass through into the Otherworld. The Egyptian goddess Meith was a magician, and her symbol was a weaver's shuttle. She was titled "The Opener of the Ways" and conducted souls to the Otherworld, following a linen thread.

This idea of following yarn into or out of the Otherworld is also found in other cultures. Ariadne, daughter of King Minos of Crete, helped her lover, the hero Theseus, find his way into the labyrinth by giving him a clew—a ball of thread (this is where our modern word *clue* comes from). Many young men and women had lost their way and their lives in the maze before him, but the magick clew unwound itself and led him to the centre of the maze where he slew the monstrous Minotaur. He then wound the yarn up to find his way out of the labyrinth.

In Greek myth, the witch goddess Hecate led the corn goddess Demeter into the underworld by means of a thread, to find her daughter Persephone (Spring).

Several fairies are said to destroy any spinning left on the wheel at Yule or Christmas. This has its origin in the fact that many sun gods and goddesses span the cosmos or the sunbeams in the hours before dawn. At Yule ("Wheel"), the Midwinter Solstice, when the sun stands still, all forms of spinning and weaving were forbidden. The Lapps forbade the turning of any kind of wheel, including cartwheels and churns.

—————— FETCHES AND CO-WALKERS ——————

There is an old conviction that everyone has a double in Fairyland that is sometimes called a co-walker, a fetch, a waff, or a reflex man. It is said that if you catch sight of this double, it is an omen of death. The Irish and the Scots would refuse to eat meat at funeral gatherings, in case this brought them into contact with their fairy double.

These ideas may go back to more ancient notions of a guardian spirit, variously called a genius by the Romans, a daemon by the Greeks, or a fylgia in Old Norse, which was rendered into English as a fetch. This appears to be part of the spirit that can act independently of the body, in the sense of an astral body, because it is said that wizards and shamans send out their fetches, often in animal forms. When this happened the shaman is normally in a trance or sleeping.

This recalls the stories of people who have been said to be in Fairyland, though their bodies remain in the mortal world—in other words, it is their spirits or fetches that visit Fairyland. In Ireland, a person who has been kidnapped by the fairies is said to be "away with the fairies" when his or her spirit may have been taken, leaving behind a passive body. This happened to Ethna, who was kidnapped by the Fairy King Finvarra. She lay with her eyes closed and never spoke a word, or smiled, or gave any sign that she knew where she was. Everyone grew sad and realized that she must have eaten fairy food. After this had gone on for a year, a voice was heard to say, "Though her body is present, her spirit is still with the fairies," and another voice answered "She will remain so forever unless her husband breaks the spell. The girdle about her waist is fastened with an enchanted pin. He should unloose it, burn the girdle, and throw its ashes before the door, then bury the enchanted pin. Only then will her spirit return from the sidhe." The young man hastily carried out these mysterious instructions, burying the pin beneath a fairy thorn. Then Ethna's soul returned to her body and the couple was truly reunited. She remembered her time in the realm of the sidhe as no more than a dream.

Such stories may be folk memories of shamanic journeys into the Otherworld, whether at will, or as part of a crisis at shamanic initiation.

ANCESTRAL SPIRITS

Some ancestral spirits remain on Earth in the form of watchers and guardians. The Celts made no distinction between the spirits of fairies and the spirits of the dead, the ancestors. Both were believed to roam the Earth and were seen feasting together. The 15th-century *Orfeo* talks of Fairyland as the Land of the Dead.[3] In the original story of Cinderella, the Fairy Godmother was the spirit of her dead mother. One young man was imprudent enough to go out on All Hallows Eve and encountered King Finvarra and his Queen Oonagh. Their company was full of merriment and passed around much food and wine, but "for all that they were the company of the dead." He recognised a neighbour who had died many years before.

A Cornishman called Noy met his dead sweetheart among the fairy hoards.[4] One day he set out for an inn but when three days had passed and he hadn't returned home, his servants went to look for him. He was discovered in a ruined barn and was amazed to discover that he had been missing for three days. He had got lost on the moor trying to take a shortcut, but had discovered a farmhouse where they were holding a Harvest Home supper. Inside hundreds of richly dressed people were feasting, but they all looked rather small. He was staggered to recognize his former sweetheart, Grace Hutchens, dead four years. He knew then that the company inside the house were fairies. Grace warned him not to touch her, eat the fairy food, or drink the cider, or he would be unable to leave. Mr. Noy believed he knew a way to rescue them both and took his hedging gloves from his pocket, turned them inside out, and threw them among the fairies, who vanished, taking Grace with them.

Every country in the world has legends of the wandering spirits of the dead, and in many places these have been incorporated into fairy lore. Some tales speak of fairies as the souls of unbaptised children, such as the Will o'the Wisp, or the Mexican Jimaninos, who dance at the Festival of the Dead. The Highland Sluagh are human souls, the hosts of the unforgiven dead, Cornish Spriggans are the ghosts of humans, and the Dunters are the souls of the victims of the Picts.

The Norse Dísir (Idis in Anglo-Saxon) was the female ancestral spirit who was honoured as a guardian of whichever person, family, or clan that lived on her territory. The Dísir were sometimes simply referred to as "dead women." She had her own shrine at the farm where prayers and offerings were made, and she was given a sacrifice every autumn, because she influenced the fertility of the land and its inhabitants. In addition, special temples called *Dísasalr* were dedicated to particular Dísir.

The Dísir appear as Fairy Godmothers or female house fairies in folklore.

Entrances to Fairyland are often said to be through burial mounds and most British, Irish, and continental fairies are said to live in the hollow hills in an underground country where the summer never ends. This is comparable with many ancient ideas of the afterlife. The Greeks believed that the souls of the good dwelt in Elysium, which means "apple-land" or "apple orchards." It was a happy realm of perpetual day, and the inhabitants could choose to be reborn on Earth wherever they elected. The Celts believed that the afterlife was lived in a permanent summer, a land of the ever young; an apple orchard where the trees were always in fruit. In Fairyland, the passage of time bears no relation to time in the real world as might be expected in a realm inhabited by souls after death.

People who are taken to Fairyland are warned not eat the food there, or they will never be able to return to the human realms. This echoes ancient Egyptian mythology, where the goddess Amenti was associated with the Land of the West, or underworld. She welcomed all deceased people to the land of the dead with bread and water. If they ate and drank they could not return to the land of the living. In Greek myth the goddess of spring, Persephone, was captured and taken to the underworld, where she ate six seeds of a pomegranate. Because of this she was forced to spend six months of each year there, which is why the Earth has winter in her absence. In Celtic lore, red food was the food of the dead and was forbidden to mankind.

The Druids taught that after death, the human soul was not extinguished, and it did not go to heaven, but instead entered into a new born baby, a newborn animal, a tree, and so on. According to Nigel Pennick:

> *"Thus the individual is not a separate being, but part of the great continuum of all things. This is expressed in the traditional relationship of humans to their* heimat, *where family, life and place are indistinguishable. The ancestral dead are part of family and place, and the non-human spirits and deities of the place acknowledged equally. The ancestors played an important role in the everyday spiritual life of the common people."*[5]

SPRITS OF PLACE

A *genius locus* is the guardian spirit or soul of a specific place. Every location has its own spirit, not only the well-known sacred sites. It was once the custom to honour these guardian spirits with offerings and seasonal rituals. As long as this happened, the spirits would remain friendly and beneficent. If they were neglected or offended, they might take their revenge. Sometimes, neglected spirits drift away, sometimes they are deliberately driven away, and when this happens the land becomes spiritually barren. Sometimes the land is inhabited by unfriendly, inimical spirits that just want to be left alone. If you enter such a place you may sense a bad atmosphere and feel decidedly unwelcome.

FAIRY LOVERS AND SWEETHEARTS

Fairies take a romantic interest in human men and women, and these relationships are fraught with danger. Fairy men may appear as strangers at village dances to make love to pretty girls. These girls will never be the same again, wasting away with longing for their absent fairy lovers. Fairy kings take women to their underground palaces but return them seven years later, prematurely old and worn out with the demands of their fairy husbands. Supernaturally beautiful fairy women call to men from the depths of the forest. Once a man has been held in the arms of his fairy sweetheart he is her slave, though she will draw his life from him, growing stronger and stronger as he grows paler and weaker. Some fairy women even suck the blood of their lovers. Water fairies and mermaids long for human men. They appear on the banks of a lake or the sea, seductively combing their golden hair. Should a man reach out to the lovely fairy, she will seize him and drag him beneath the waves, drowning him and stealing his soul to keep in a lobster pot.

Garconer is an Irish elf who looks like a handsome gypsy, with bright black eyes and black curly hair. His name means "love talker" and he loves to seduce mortal women, but any woman who yields to his sweet words and kisses is lost; she will pine away and die when he leaves—and he always does leave.

The Leanan Sidhe ("fairy sweetheart") is a Celtic fairy, of either sex, who seeks the love of mortals. If the mortal refuses, then the fairy must become their slave. However, if the mortal consents, he or she is bound to the fairy and cannot escape, except by finding another to take his or her place. As a lover, the Leanan Sidhe is very passionate, but his or her human partner pays the price of the relationship with a short life. The embrace of the fairy draws life and breath from them while the fairy becomes bright and strong. This is particularly true in the case of the Isle of Man Lhiannan Shee, who is more like a vampire who sucks the life from her lover. Those she favours have brilliant careers, but die young.

However, some marriages with fairies work out well. In the Orkneys, Magnus O'Kierfea took a fairy bride in addition to his own mortal wife. On festival nights such as Halloween, Christmas, and New Year's Eve he would be sure to set a place for her and the food would always be gone in the morning. With her aid he became a famous healer and they had three daughters. Kirwan of Castle Hackett in Connaught are also married a fairy. A fairy king asked his aid against a hostile fairy tribe that had invaded his territories. Kirwan was pleased to have such a powerful ally and agreed to help, and men and fairies together defeated the enemy. The Connaught men were rewarded with presents of gold and silver while Kirwan received a fairy bride. All of his female descendants were noted for their unearthly beauty.

Relationships between humans and fairies always have conditions and taboos imposed on them, such as the fairy should never be struck or touched with iron, or seen on a certain day. Should the fairy lover leave for any reason, usually because of the breaking of a taboo, then the human spouse will pine away and die.

According to one Welsh fairy legend, a young man was grazing his cattle on the banks of Llyn y Fan Fach when he saw a lovely fairy maiden sitting on the shore, combing her hair. He thought that he had never seen a woman as beautiful and tried to entice her to come to him by offering her gifts of bread. She smiled and shook her head, but this only made him more determined. Eventually, after many attempts, he persuaded the fairy to marry him. She warned him that if he should strike her more than twice, she would vanish forever. As her dowry, her father bestowed upon the couple many fairy sheep, goats, and cows, which all emerged from the lake at the call of the fairy woman. The couple was married, and for many years lived happily on a small farm near Myddfai, and had three handsome sons. One day, the couple were preparing to go to a Christening, and the man asked his fairy wife to get the pony, while he fetched something from the house. On returning, he found her still standing in the same spot. Fearing they would be late, he tapped his wife on the shoulder and told her to hurry up. She turned and looked at him with a sad expression, for he had struck her once. A few months later they went to a wedding, and the fairy burst into tears. Embarrassed, the man struck her on the shoulder and bade her be quiet. She turned to him and said, "I am weeping because their troubles are just beginning, and so are ours, for you have struck the second blow." This frightened the farmer, and he took care not to strike his wife again in the years that passed, until one day they attended a funeral and his wife burst out laughing. Enraged, he tapped her on the shoulder and asked what was the matter with her. She replied that "When people die, their troubles are over, and so is our marriage, for you have struck the third blow." With that, she disappeared into the lake, taking all her fairy animals with her. The farmer never saw her again.

7
Fairy Etiquette

airies do not always welcome the attentions of human beings. They hate idle curiosity and selfish demands. When you deal with fairies you must treat them with respect and prove that you are worthy to treat with them. You cannot make them obey you at will. They are not there to teach you as you demand and certainly not to serve you and grant your wishes. They simply exist and have their own objectives and schedules.

In order to gain the friendship of the fairies you must take certain steps. Fairies appreciate being treated with consideration. It is wise to create a warm, tidy place by the hearth for them and leave the fire smouldering at night. When you go to bed, put out water for them to wash in, and wine or milk to drink—or better still, a bowl of best cream. Leave the last apples on the tree for them and the last grain in the barrel, or the last few drops of milk in the pail. These are ancient ways of making offerings to the spirits that surround us. Though in practice, the food and drink are often eaten by the wild animals, it is understood that the spirits first take nourishment from it.

The first milk from the cow should always be spilt on the ground as libation for the fairies. Milk is one of their favourite foods. Some fairies keep herds of magickal cows that give unlimited supplies of milk. Others steal milk from mortal cows. In some areas, milk was poured into stone hollows near the dairy as an offering to the fairies. A good Irish housewife would always leave out a dish of milk or cream for the fairies and never completely drain the churn or milk pail, as the dregs were the prerogative of the little people. One fairy mother was overheard to say that she would knock over the milk pail so that her child could drink its fill. In ancient times, milk was sacred, a symbol of feminine care and sustenance, and associated with many goddesses personified as nurturing mothers. The stars were thought to be drops of milk from the breasts of a goddess and this is how the Milky Way got its name; the Celts called it "The Track of the White Cow."

It was considered very important to retain the goodwill of the fairies, and careless talk about them was to be avoided, particularly out of doors, for the wind would carry anything that was said to fairy ears. Remember that fairies don't like being spoken of by name and don't like being called "fairies." It is better to call them "The Gentry," "the Good Neighbours," the "Kindly Ones," or some such flattery. There is an ancient belief that by naming something you invoke it. The true name of something encapsulates its essential nature; people, animals, places, gods, and spirits have real names that are secret. If a person can discover the real name then he or she will have that being in his or her power, and the real name can be used to work magick against its owner. Magicians use words of power, which include the names of gods and spirits, tapping into the essence and energy of the being when the name is intoned correctly.

This belief is exemplified in many fairy tales, when the secret name of a fairy is discovered and it loses its power. A miller foolishly bragged to the king that his daughter was so clever that she could spin straw into gold. The avaricious king immediately locked the girl into a room with a spinning wheel and a pile of straw, warning her that if she failed to produce the gold promised by her father she should be put to death. As the girl cried out in despair—for her father's claim was nothing more than an idle boast—a dwarf appeared and offered to perform the task in return for her necklace. She agreed and he span the straw into threads of the finest gold.

The king was both amazed and delighted. He locked the girl into a larger room with more straw, again with the injunction that should she fail to spin the gold she would be put to death. Again the dwarf appeared and span the gold in return for the girl's ring.

Inevitably, the king showed the maiden into a yet larger room, filled with yet more straw. This time he informed her that should she fail to turn the straw into gold she would die, but should she succeed he would make her his wife. The dwarf appeared, but the girl was out of jewellery, and instead he exacted a promise that when she became queen her first child should be given to him.

The king married the maiden and a year later their first child was born. Even before the Christening, the dwarf appeared, demanding his fee: the royal prince-ling. The queen began to weep and the dwarf seemed to relent, saying that if she could guess his name within three days, she should keep the baby.

Though she guessed many names and servants were sent out to discover more, none proved to be the name of the dwarf. On the last night she began to despair until a messenger informed her he had overheard a little man singing a rhyme about his name being Rumpelstiltskin. When the dwarf returned the queen was able to tell him his name waw "Rumpelstiltskin." The thwarted manni-kin, in his fury, stamped his foot so deep into the ground that he tore himself in half.

Fairies will always reward a good deed or kindness shown towards them as in the following story:

One day a man was working in the fields when he heard the fairies talking over their baking; they said they had no peel, a long-handled shovel for taking the bread in and out of the oven. The man thought to himself that he would make one for them. He left it out in the field where they could find it, and the next day it was gone. In return, the fairies had left him a batch of wonderful cakes.

Fairies sometimes borrow from humans without ask-ing first. A farmer called John Fraser prospered for a time and supplied milk of excellent quality to his Inverness customers. Suddenly, the cows stopped giv-ing milk, and this continued for an entire year. Then Fraser was standing near a rowan tree when he saw a strange dwarfish man approaching. He had flowing brown hair, which contrasted strangely with his wrinkled and aged face. He carried a long, tapering sapling of hawthorn that seemed to be pulled down at one end by some invisible burden. Neither man spoke, but Fraser suspected that the stranger had some evil intent, and acting on instinct, he seized the end of the hawthorn, and cut it off with his knife. The old man seemed unaware, but from the cut twig that had fallen, a stream of rich, creamy milk flowed. This was the milk the fairies had "borrowed" from his cows for the past few months.

However, should a mortal borrow fairy utensils or food he will cause offense if he tries to return more than he borrowed, while fairies always return favours with a bonus. Fairies always return two measures of barleymeal for one of oatmeal, and if this is kept in a place by itself it proves an inexhaustible supply, providing the bottom of the vessel is never made to appear, no questions asked, and no blessing pronounced over it. At the 13th-century church at Frensham in Surrey there is a huge cauldron that local people say was borrowed from the fairies, but never returned. For this reason, the fairies would never lend the village anything again.

Take care to be kind to travellers, for they may be fairy princes in disguise. A fairy may appear in the guise of an old woman or poor man and ask you to share your food, take them to their destination, or even mend their broken wheelbarrow. If you pass the test the fairy may reveal hidden treasure, show you how to cast spells, reveal the power of herbs, save your life, or make someone love you. A sudden stroke of luck may fall upon you or your family.

However, do not say "thank you," as they will be offended. Do not offer them clothes as a gift or try to return more than is given or lent. Never mention what the fairies have done for you or speak of your relationship with the fairies, or they will turn against you. Never discuss your dealings with fairies with others. This is very important. It is between you and them. Other people may not understand, and you might be giving away your power and secrets.

Fairy blessings can be conferred on those mortals that the fairies take a liking to. They may protect their favourites from harm or give them great riches, beauty, or magickal powers. Fairies like simple, unpretentious, sincere folk and hate the nosy, boastful, quarrelsome, and greedy. They detest people who give themselves airs and pretend to be what they are not. Fairies also love beauty and luxury and hate people who are mean and parsimonious.[1] Fairies hate greed. The struggle for gain and excessive possessions has no place in the lives of those who seek to work with fairies, and the legends of fairies are full of warnings on this subject: There was a Scottish farmer of Auchriachan who was one day looking after his goats at Glenlivet when a thick fog came down and confused him, so that he became lost and wandered about till it started to get dark. He expected to die in the cold night, but then ahead of him he saw a light. He made his way towards it and found himself in a wild and lonely place, where he thought he might have been the first human to ever tread. Still, he advanced towards an open door and was surprised to find that the housekeeper who greeted him was an old friend of his, recently deceased. She ran to him in some agitation, and told him to hide himself in a corner, or he would be lost. Scarcely had he concealed himself when a host of fairies entered, calling loudly for food and asking what there was to eat.

An old elf, seated by the fire, said, "You know that old farmer of Auchriachan, who we all hate for his greed and miserliness? He never gives us anything, and deprives us of our proper due. He doesn't even leave the gleaning in the fields for us; his mother was a witch and taught him charms against us. Well, tonight he is away from home, looking for his goats, our allies, and we can go and take his ox for our supper!" All the rest agreed most readily, "Yes, Thomas Rhymer is right, that farmer is a wretched miser, but where shall we get some bread to go with it?"

"We'll take his new-baked bread as well! His wife forgot to put the sign of the cross on it, so it will be easy." The miserable farmer heard himself discussed and saw his ox brought in, killed, and cooked. While the fairies were busy with the feast, the housekeeper found an opportunity to smuggle him out of the fairy dwelling. The fog had cleared and a bright moon shone, so that he was able to find his way home without difficulty.

His wife was overjoyed to see him, as she had been very worried. She brought him milk and cheese, but he knew that the fairies had stolen the substance of it and would not touch it. He asked after his ox, and if his wife had used the usual protection from fairies. She replied that, in her fear for him, she had forgotten. "Alas," he cried, my favourite ox is gone!" "What do you mean?" she asked, "I saw it not an hour ago, standing in the byre." "That was only a false semblance of it," he replied. "The fairies have taken it. Bring the false ox here so that I might get rid of it quickly." So saying, he aimed a blow at the head of the ox, which fell down. No cat or dog or other thing would eat it, or even go near it.[2]

Nothing must be taken away from Fairyland, should you be lucky enough to visit it. Fairies take a very dim view of this, and you would be fortunate to escape with nothing more than being barred from Fairyland forever: A man of Zahren, in Mecklenburg, was seized with thirst on his way home when he heard music in a barrow known to be the haunt of the fairy folk. People were then on familiar terms with the fairy folk; and the man cried out and asked for a drink. His appeal was at once answered by the appearance of a little fellow with a flask of delicious wine. After slaking his thirst the man took the opportunity to make off with the flask; but he was pursued by the whole troop of elves, only one of whom succeeded in keeping up with him—and he had only one leg. The thief, however, managed to get over a crossroads where One-leg could not follow him; and the latter then, making a virtue of necessity, cried out:

"Thou mayst keep the flask; and henceforth always drink thereout, for it will never be empty; but beware of looking into it." For some years the elf's injunction was observed; but one day, in a fit of curiosity, the peasant looked into the bottom of the flask, and there sat a horrid toad! The toad disappeared, and so did the liquor; and the man, in a short time, fell miserably sick.

A Swedish tradition relates that, one night of Christmas in the year 1490, one of the serving-men of the lady of

Liungby, in Scania, rode out to inquire the cause of the noise at the Magle Stone. He found the trolls dancing and making merry. A fair troll woman stepped forth and offered him a drinking horn and a pipe, praying he would drink to the troll king's health and blow in the pipe. He snatched the horn and pipe from her, and spurring back to the mansion, delivered them into his lady's hands. The trolls followed and begged to have their treasures back, promising prosperity to the lady's race if she would restore them. She kept them, however; and they are said to be still preserved at Liungby as memorials of the adventure. But the serving-man who took them died three days after, and the horse on the second day; the mansion has been twice burnt, and the family never prospered after.

Iron terrifies fairies. Show them any kind of iron and they will vanish immediately. If you want to work with fairies, you must keep iron and steel from your person and circle. The idea of witches using steel athames is a very recent one and comes from the pages of ritual magick grimoires, rather than tradition. I only ever use a bronze knife for delineating sacred places or cutting herbs for magickal use. A flint knife would work equally well and will be sharper than steel.

To protect yourself, your family, and your property from the unwanted attentions of evil or mischievous fairies keep a knife or a nail in your pocket and under your pillow at night. A horseshoe hung over the door will keep fairies and other spirits out. However, unlike other fairies, dwarfs are smiths and can work in iron with complete impunity. The tradition that iron gives protection from fairies may have sprung from some dim memory of the Celtic invasions. The Celts were armed with iron, while the aboriginal races they defeated had weapons of bronze or stone. Elf-bolts, the flint darts commonly found in Britain, Ireland, and Continental Europe often ascribed to fairies and witches, are actually Stone Age Man's flint arrow heads.

Solitary fairies such as brownies and house fairies are often ragged in appearance, but they are offended by gifts of clothes and will promptly disappear forever if given a new suit, so if you have a helpful fairy don't be tempted to reward it in this fashion. You can make use of your own clothes to free yourself from fairy enchantments. If fairies are troubling you at night, place your shoes with the toes pointing outwards by the bed and throw your socks under it. If you are being pixy-led (tricked from your path by fairies) turn your clothes inside out and this will confuse the fairies long enough to allow you to make your escape. A glove thrown into a fairy ring will enable a mortal trapped in it to make his or her escape.

The ability to change shape or become invisible often depends on donning or removing some article of clothing. For example, the selkies assume sealskins to swim in the sea and shed them when they come ashore. If these skins are hidden from them they cannot resume their seal shape or return to the water, and must abide as a human on land. Wearing animal skins takes on an extra dimension in shamanic practice, when wearing the skin of a creature indicates assuming some of its powers.

Many fairies are naked and prefer to stay that way, being completely unselfconscious about their undressed state. They don't share humans' prudery about nudity and implied sin that the bible claims descended on Adam and Eve when they were expelled from the Garden of Eden. It can be implied that fairies inhabit a more natural, innocent, and freer realm of consciousness.

Fairies can bestow any skill they wish on their favourites. One skill frequently granted is that of piping or fiddling. There were three McCrimmon brothers and two of them were great pipers, and used to go piping about everywhere, but they just kept the youngest at home to do all the house and fieldwork. When the Highland Games were due, the youngest one asked if he might go, too, to hear the piping, but the elder two went off and left him watching the cows. He was feeling very sorry for himself when a little green man came and asked what the matter was. The boy explained that he had wanted to go to the Games and hear the piping. "I'll give you a piping," said the fairy, and he played the loveliest tune the young man had ever heard. "Now you play," the fairy said.

"I can't play," the boy replied, "and furthermore, my brothers have locked me out of the house so I can't get at the pipes."

"That's no problem," the fairy declared, "just blow in the lock, and put your little finger in and turn it." The boy did as he was told and the door opened. "Look in the old chest," said the fairy, "and you will find your pipes." There was an old chest there he had never seen before. He opened it, and not only was there a set of pipes mounted in gold, but also the finest kilt imaginable. The boy put it on and looked very smart. "Play a tune on your pipes," said the fairy. The boy took up the pipes and a tune formed of its own accord. The fairy told him it was called *The Finger Lock*. He went off to the games and played the tune, and everyone was enchanted by it, and he took first prize. That was how *The Finger Lock* was first played.

Fairies, particularly water fairies, have the power to make human beings into great healers. The lake fairy of Llyn y Fan Fach might have left her husband when he broke the taboos surrounding their marriage, but she returned occasionally to instruct her sons in the art of herbs and medicine. They became the famous physicians of Myddfai.

Fairies teach witches how to use herbs, because they know all their healing properties. For example, the Seefräuline, a German lake maiden, and the Vile pass on the knowledge of forest herbs. The Auki, a Peruvian mountain fairy, helps shamans with healing.

The *Ceaird Chomuinn* ("Association Craft") can be bestowed by fairies on those they like. A boy apprenticed to carpentry was working with his master on building a boat. He found he had forgotten a tool and ran back to the workshop to fetch it, but disturbed a crowd of fairies hard at work on carpentry. They scattered as he ran in, and one little fairy woman was so flustered that she dropped her silk girdle as she ran, and the boy picked it up and put it in his pocket. In a minute, the little woman came back to look for it and asked the boy to give it to her. He refused, and she promised to give him full skill in his trade without further apprentice-ship, so he restored it to her, and she ran away with it happily. Next morning the boy got up very early and fitted two planks into the boat so perfectly that the master asked him if he knew who had been there, for they were set in by a master who could teach him his trade. So the boy told the master his story, and his skill stayed with him all his life, in spite of his mention of a fairy gift.

To form a bond with an Otherworldly being means to participate in an equal exchange. You can achieve this reciprocity by protecting the environment, clean-ing a fairy habitat, or something much more profound.

UNFRIENDLY FAIRIES

Making friends with fairies doesn't always work; sometimes they may be inadvertently offended. Some are simply inimical to human beings, or their normal courses may seem cruel or malicious to the outsider. There are certainly darker beings—embodiments of the powers of death, dissolution, illness, blight, and despair. They are not "evil" as we might understand it, and have their place in the cosmos, but they are dangerous to deal with. Just as there are malicious humans there are malicious spirits, practical jokers, and those who ap-pear in the guise of helper only to trick you.

If you are feeling malice, envy, anger, or despair when you call up the spirits, you'll invoke a spirit that mirrors these qualities. Unpleasant spirits are attracted to people who are very negative and are nourished by this negativity. They are attracted to people with alcohol or drug problems, and feed off the aura generated by the addiction. You may become tired and listless under the attention of such spirits.

The Anglo-Saxons, among others, thought that various fairies were the spirits of different diseases. In Norway, people feared the elf wind or *alvgest,* which is the breath of elves and which covers the body of a person with blisters. In England, paralysis was believed to be caused by the invisible presence of a fairy market. Tuberculosis was caused by eating fairy food or by visiting a fairy hill at night. Fairies inflicted impetigo and lice. Rheumatism, cramps, and bruising were a punishment for annoying the fairies.

The small flint arrowheads, made by Stone-Age man, were once thought to have been manufactured by fairies and were called "elf-bolts," "elf-arrows," or "elf-shot." The elves and fairies were thought to use them to cause harm, propelling them into humans or livestock. Isobel Gowdie, the Scottish witch, said *"...as for elf arrows-heads the devil shapes them with his own hand and so delivers them to the elf boys."* Deaths were attributed to them and it was thought they could induce paralysis; the origin of the word *stroke* for paralysis is derived from "elf-stroke."

If you can find an elf-bolt it is a lucky charm and will guard against any further attacks by elf-bolts. It can also cure wounds when rubbed on them. You should never give an elf-bolt away, however, as this will be an invitation for the fairies to kidnap you.

There are other fairy objects that are lucky charms if they are found. A substance called "elf's blood" (*fuil siochaire*) may be found on the shores of the Hebrides. It looks like a holed stone and is half-red and half-black. The fairy spade (*caibe sith*) is a smooth slippery black stone shaped like the sole of a shoe. It can be put in water, which is reputed to cure sick people and cattle. The small, round fossil called an *echinite* is known as a Fairy Loaf.

Fairies are known to be thieves, but when they take something they take only its substance or spirit, so when a cow is elf-taken it appears to be struck down by some disease. It will lie down and refuse to get up. Though it will continue to eat, it will produce no milk. When it dies its flesh will turn out to be a stock of alder wood or some rubbish.

Fairies can also steal the spirit of the land itself. When this happens the fields appear to yield a crop but the ears of corn will not fill out, the harvest will be slender and the animal fodder without nourishment.

Fairies can only take away what selfish humans deserve to lose. If you "over look a child" (that is, look on it with envy) then the fairies have it in their power. When people become miserly and refuse to share their possessions or do not value them, the fairies will take the goodness out of them. When a farmer grumbles about his crop, even if it is good, the fairies will take the substance out of it. When you mislay something and can't find it, no matter how hard you look, it is almost certain that the fairies have taken it.

There are guardians who protect places. You may unintentionally have triggered one of these guardians by treading in a sacred place, by polluting the place or by awakening it with unwonted magickal practices or spiritual practices. A member of my coven once had trouble with a guardian spirit, awoken when she crossed a particular path in a particular negative mood. It had been set up as a magickal sentinel to a secret sacred site. It manifested in the form of a bull-headed man, with cloven feet, for weeks afterwards; the cloven feet could be heard echoing on the pathway. It started following her home, and her flatmate was aware that the temperature of the flat had fallen, they both began having nightmares, and eventually I had to appease the spirit.

It is possible that your path has crossed that of a fairy about its own business, and it is annoyed by this.

——— PROTECTION AGAINST FAIRIES ———

If you are being troubled by fairies, you should keep a piece of iron about you. (An old nail or a knife would work). Hang a horseshoe over your door to keep out evil spirits.

Fairies can pixy-lead travellers—that is, they can get them lost whatever path they take and no matter how well they think they know the road. A remedy against this is to turn your clothes inside out; as explained previously, this will confuse the fairies long enough to allow you to make your escape. If a friend has been dragged into a fairy ring, remember to toss one of your gloves inside and the revellers will disperse.

If you are having nightmares, place a piece of iron under your pillow. Alternatively, you can scatter flax on the bedroom floor, which will confuse the fairies who cause the bad dreams, and place your shoes with the toes pointing away from the bed.

A rowan cross tied with red thread will offer protection when hung in a high place in the house or byre. The besom or broom can be placed beside the hearth to prevent fairies coming down the chimney. A Witch Bottle (a glass bottle containing sharp objects such as nails and pins, ashes, salt, and rowan wood) can be buried before the doorstep.

Because they are connected with the Old Religion, fairies dislike Christian symbols. They run from bibles and crucifixes, and drawing a cross on cakes will stop fairies dancing on them. Churchyard mold scattered on the doorstep will keep fairies out. Church bells scare away fairies. After Halloween (October 31st) any crops left in the fields belong to the fairies, so bells used to be tolled all day on October 30th to make sure the little folk did not pre-empt their prerogative while the harvesters hurried to finish their work. The bells on Morris Men's costumes offer them protection from fairies and other spirits.

Fairies don't like to catch sight of themselves in mirrors, so a mirror facing any point where they might enter a house, such as opposite a door or window, will deter them.

Fire is the great preventative against fairy magick. Carry a burning candle or charcoal block around a person or place troubled by malicious spirits.

There are a wide variety of plants that protect against the attentions of fairies. Trailing pearlwort (known in Gaelic as *mothan* or *moan*) protects its possessor from fire and the attacks of fairy women. If fairies are stealing your milk, lace it with *moan* and it will render them powerless, as the *Flora Scotica* states:

"So long as I preserve the Moan
There lives not on earth
One who will take my cow's milk from me."

St. John's Wort (in Gaelic *achlasan challumchile*) wards off fevers and prevents the fairies from carrying off people while they sleep. A twig of broom will keep fairies out of the house, while a gorse hedge will keep them off your property. In Scotland, heather is used to keep fairies and ghosts out of the house.

An Anglo-Saxon remedy involves rubbing myrrh into wine with an equal amount of white incense (frankincense). Shave a little off an agate and add it to the wine. Drink after fasting for three, nine, or 12 mornings.

Burning thorns on a fairy hill releases captive children. Parents should adorn their children with bells or daisy chains to protect children on May Eve. A mulberry tree in your garden will keep away fairies. At the dangerous times of Midsummer and Midwinter you should dance around it counterclockwise. This is the origin of the rhyme "Here we go Round the Mulberry Bush."

Ground ivy (*Glechoma hederacea*) is a magick charm against the unwanted attentions of fairies. One story tells of a young girl who was seized by fairies who tried to get her to join in their revels and drink their wine. She was saved by a red-haired man who led her out and gave her a branch of *Athair-Luzz* (Gaelic for ground-ivy) and told her to hold it in her hand till she got home, then no one could hurt her. She took it and ran home, though she heard pursuing footsteps. When she reached home she bolted the door and heard voices saying, "The power we had over you is gone through the magick of the herb—but when you dance again with us on the hill, you will stay with us forever more, and none shall hinder." She kept the herb safe and the fairies troubled her no more, but for a long time she heard the fairy music.

Salve to Remove Elf Banes

Equal parts of:

Hop flowers

Wormwood

Bishop's wort

Lupine

Vervain

Henbane

Harewort

Viper's bugloss

Heathberry shoots

Leek

Garlic

Cleaver's seeds

Fennel seeds or leaves

Method: Put the herbs in a pan with enough fat to cover them. You can used butter, lard, or petroleum jelly. Simmer over a low heat for 30 minutes. Strain through muslin and anoint any affected parts. (**Note:** Some people are allergic to certain herbs. Please consult an herbal practitioner before using.)

8
Elementals

Earth my body,
Water my blood,
Air my breath,
and Fire my spirit

T he ancient Greeks debated the composition of the world. Thales, looking around and seeing the plentiful nature of water, considered that it was the basic element of creation. In contrast, Heraclitus concluded it was fire, and Anaxagoras thought it must be air. The first person to suggest that the world was created from four Elements—Earth, Air, Fire, and Water—was Empedocles in the sixth century C.E. These were not Elements as we think of them in modern scientific terms, but four basic qualities that are embodied within everything that is manifest. Following this theory, the Neoplatonists, in the third century C.E. spoke of spirits associated with each of the Elements and divided them into four classes, each associated with one of the Elements. However, it was the 16th-century alchemist, doctor, and philosopher Paracelsus who gave these "Elementals" their familiar names.[1] He called the spirits of the earth Gnomes, the spirits of the Air Sylphs, spirits of Fire Salamanders, and Water spirits Undines.

According to Paracelsus, while Sylphs and Undines are kindly disposed towards humans, Salamanders cannot be approached or approach humans, and Gnomes are usually malevolent. However, Gnomes can be persuaded to become servants to a magician and *"if you do your duty to him, he will do his duty to you."* He went on to say that Elementals hate dogmatists, sceptics, drunkards, gluttons, and the quarrelsome, while they love natural, child-like, innocent, and sincere people. *"...[To] him who binds or pledges himself to them they give knowledge and riches enough. They know our minds and thoughts also, so that they may be easily influenced to come to us."*

Paracelsus declared that while man is made of three substances—the spiritual, the astral, and terrestrial—Elementals live exclusively in only one of the Elements. They occupy a position between men and pure spirits, though they have blood and bones, and they eat and sleep and mate and produce offspring. They live in dwellings that are made of special materials *"as different from the substances we know as the web of a spider is different from our linen."*

The powers and influences of each the four Elements are embodied in its Elementals. Elementals are specialized spirits concerned with their own spheres of influence, and have no special interest in human affairs. Though the Water Elementals may be involved in floods, they do not cause them out of malice to the people affected by it. Air spirits may be involved in hurricanes and tornadoes, and are simply going about their own business, and this is part of the natural world, however inconvenient or dangerous it might be for humans.

Witches and Pagans work with Elementals, inviting them into the circle or ritual space. One of the basic principles that any witch or shaman learns is that almost everything in the cosmos is made up of some combination of the four Elements. If you can know the four Elements directly, then you can understand anything in the cosmos.

Working with Elementals is fraught with danger, and they must be treated with the utmost respect. Any requests for their help must be carefully phrased, because they tend to take things literally, and properly directed to the correct type of Elemental. Earth Elementals are concerned with the physical world, with growth, formation, strength, and health. Earth Elemental magick might include working with plants, crystals, gardens, and the wildwood. Air Elementals are concerned with movement, communication, the psychic senses, inspiration, and the powers of the intellect. Fire Elementals are concerned with passion, transformation, purification, and energy. Water Elementals are concerned with the ebb and flow, with tranquillity, purification, cleansing, scrying, and the emotions. The most usual representation for the Elemental in ritual is a stone for the Earth Elemental, a feather or incense for the Air Elemental, a candle for the Fire Elemental, and a cauldron of water for the Water Elemental.

WATER ELEMENTALS

Every body of water, from the smallest stream to the vast ocean, has its own protective fairy, living below the surface. In Wales, fairy maidens called the Gwragedd Annwn dwell beneath the lakes. They are exceedingly beautiful and occasionally venture ashore to take human lovers and husbands. One such Lady of the Lake, called

Vivienne or Nimue, appears in the stories of King Arthur, supplying him with Excalibur, a magickal fairy sword.

The sea is as densely populated with fairies as any place on earth. In its depths, dwell mermaids and mermen, nymphs, and others. These spirits control the weather and the water, raise storms, and have the power to cause a shipwreck or keep a ship safe. In ancient times, it was the practice to placate the spirits of the sea with a sacrifice before setting out on a voyage.

Like the sea, many sea fairies are personified as lovely and seductive, but treacherous. The best known of these is the mermaid. It is possible that the legend of the mermaid has its origins in the goddesses who rose from the sea, such as Venus/Aphrodite, or the fish-tailed Atargatis and Derceto. The sea is associated with the Great Mother Goddess whose names include Maia, Mary, Mara, Marian, Maria, and Miriam; all names are derived from a root word for sea. Sea goddesses are usually also goddesses of love and the moon, drawing the tides, rivers, dew, and flow of human life. Ancient mariners would have a tattoo of a star to honour the goddess Venus as they steered by her star. She was also the prototype of the ship figureheads.

Some water fairies are unfriendly and dangerous. Jenny Greenteeth lives in the River Ribble in Northern England. When green weeds wave in the flowing water, it is a sign that Jenny is lurking beneath the surface, ready to take another victim. She haunts the stepping stones near Brungerley and every seven years claims a human life by grabbing some hapless traveller and pulling him beneath the water to drown. Children are warned not to go near the water, or Jenny Greenteeth will take them.

Jenny is only one such fairy. Another is Peg Prowler who haunts the River Tees. She is also green with long hair and sharp teeth. If people wade in the water she pulls on their ankles and drags them down to drown. Peg also demands the sacrifice of a life every seven years, but will be satisfied with a small animal or bird, though if this is not offered she will take a human life.

The Powers of Water

Water has often been considered to be a living thing, or certainly to have the power of sustaining, bestowing and even restoring life—as well as being capable of taking it. Every ancient society honoured springs, wells, and water sources as sacred. The Celts and others sacrificed treasure to lake and river spirits. Rivers were worshipped by the Druids and were believed to each have their resident water spirits that required sacrifices to be made to them. The River Tweed is said to demand a yearly sacrifice, but the Till is more voracious:

> *Tweed says to Till,*
> *"What gars ye Tin sae still?"*
> *Says Till to Tweed,*
> *"Though ye run Wi' speed, and I Tin slaw,*
> *Whaurye droon ae man,*
> *I droon twa."*

Just as water takes the form of whatever it is poured into, water fairies have the power to alter their shapes. If you anger them by polluting their water, they may appear as hideous, green toothed hags to drench you with a sudden storm, or drown you beneath the waves. If they take a liking to you, they might appear as gorgeous, golden haired youths or maids, wooing you with sweet fairy music. A "prototype" of Water fairies is the Greek sea god Proteus, known as The Old Man of the Sea, who is the most masterful shapeshifter of all. He is able to assume any shape he desires. Most water fairies are said to be shapeshifters, perhaps because of the fluid and changeable nature of water itself, which is only given shape by the vessel that holds it.

Water is liquid, like the blood that flows through our veins. Water can manifest in a drop of dew, a gentle rain to the raging flood or the crash of the ocean wave. A trickle of water will eventually wear away a mountain. All life started in the rich biological soup of the oceans, just as the uterine waters of your mother's womb protected you. It is associated with emotions and feelings, the subconscious mind. Water can be the safety of the uterine waters of the womb, the cleansing stream, the deep pool of the subconscious mind, the nourishing river, the brew of initiation, the movement of the tides, and the power of the sea to give bounty or destroy with its tempest.

Water is a universal symbol of cleansing and regeneration. Some water has healing powers, such as the Chalice Well in Glastonbury. Water heals, especially water flowing east to west, is empowered by the rising sun at the Vernal Equinox, May Day, and Midsummer. Any stream that runs north to south has magickal properties as does the place where two streams meet; these were often the places for magick and Otherworld contact. Pools and lakes are magickal entrances to the Otherworld. Where three streams meet was always considered to be a especially potent place for magick where people gathered to drink the water as it had miraculous properties.

Water is ruled by the moon, which pulls the ebb and flow of the tides, and many water fairies are said to appear by moonlight. Under the full moon is the best time to contact them. Our bodies too respond to the moon's tides, as they are mainly water. We are influenced by the moon tides almost as much as Water Elementals are, though more subtly.

Water relates to the ebb and flow of events, the natural tides of life. Water fairies know about the emotions, love and the spiritual side of love. Water fairies help us overcome emotional hurts and restrictions, because they are fluid.

People with a lot of water in the psychological make-up can be idealistic, romantic, psychic, artistic, poetic, nurturing, and imaginative. However, they can also be self-involved, vapid, avaricious, ruthless, indecisive, manipulative, weak, over emotional, and impractical.

The Correspondences of Water

Symbols: cup, cauldron, bowl of water, seashells.
Colours: blue, sea green, grey, silver.
Direction: west.
Season: autumn.
Time: twilight.
Life Tide: old age.
Magickal Influences: intuition, insight, fertility, divination, love, emotions.
Gems: aquamarine, azurite, beryl, celestite, chrysocolla, coral, quartz crystal, moonstone, mother-of-pearl, pearl, sapphire, selenite.

Quality: emotion, feeling.

Vowel Sound: O.

Sense: taste.

Key Words: culmination, harvest, flowing, nourishing, love, intuition, emotions, feelings, intuition, compassion, empathy, sympathy, devotion, quest, aspiration, harmony, beauty, serenity, fluidity, joy.

Herbs: lemon balm, eucalyptus, gardenia, iris, calamus, camomile, jasmine, lemon, lotus, myrrh, orris, rose, sandalwood, thyme.

Animals: fish, dolphins, water creatures.

Water Elemental Spells and Rituals

Baths and Showers

You can use the power of the water in your home when you wash the dishes or when you take your daily bath or shower. Treat it as an opportunity to attune to the water spirits and their power of cleansing. You can stand in the shower and feel the water wash away all the stresses of the day, all the negative thought and experiences and even the pains of your body. Let them wash down the drain.

In addition there are some bath treats that combine the powers of water with those of herbs:

Bath to Relax and Revive

1/2 oz. chamomile flowers

1/2 oz. lavender flowers

1/2 oz. lemon balm leaves

1/2 oz. white willow bark

1 pint water

Method: Simmer the willow bark in the water for 15 minutes. Remove from the heat and add the flowers. Infuse 10 minutes, strain, and add 1 cup to the bathwater.

Purification Bath

1 lb. salt

a few drops rosemary oil

a few drops frankincense oil

a few drops lavender oil

Method: Blend together and store in an airtight container.

Healing Bath Salt

1 lb. sea salt

1 oz. lavender flowers

1/2 oz. rose petals

chopped orange peel

1/2 oz. rosemary leaves, chopped

a few drops mandarin oil

Method: Blend together and store in an airtight container for a moon before using to develop the scent.

Crystal Water

To connect with the spirits of water, strongest at full moon, place spring water in a glass jar with a quartz crystal and put it out in the light of the full moon. It must be left outside with the lid off so the moonbeams can touch the water. Take it in before the sun comes up, as

you want it charged with moon energy. Drink
the water (within three days of making) before
undertaking meditations or ritual concerned with
Water Elementals.

Thunderstorm Water

Collect water during a thunderstorm and use
it for breaking bad luck and deadlocked situa-
tions. Drink the water and ask the storm spirits
to bring you new insights in your meditation or
in your dreams.

Thunderstorm Talisman Charging

Storms are times of powerful energy. Charge
any talismans you have made, particularly those
made of oak, ash, or hawthorn, or dedicated in
the names of Thor, Thunor, Tan, Odin, Woden,
Zeus, or Jupiter, during a thunderstorm.

Rainmaking Spell

Cut and burn fern leaves to attract rain.

Rainwater Protection Spell

Money washed in rainwater cannot be
stolen.

Scrying Bowl

Scry comes from the Anglo-Saxon *descry* and
means "to see." It is a very ancient form of divination and makes use of mirrors, crystal balls,
or, as in this case, a bowl of water. Fill a dark
bowl with water. Light a white candle so that it

illuminates the water. Drop some olive oil into the water and gaze into it. Let the blankness of the water help to clear your mind. If you can manage this, images will begin to form between your mind's eye and the surface of the water. The secret with scrying is not to try too hard to see images within the surface.

Scrying With Moon and Cauldron

You can ask the Water spirits to help you with this divination. Fill a cauldron with water. Allow the moonlight to be reflected in it and gaze at the pictures, clearing your mind. Visions may then appear on the surface of the water.

Water and Wax Divination

Drop hot wax from a candle into cold water. Shapes will form; try to read from the patterns. A hand might symbolize a gift; a bird, a message; a heart, love, for example, but as in all these cases, use you own intuition to interpret the messages.

Water as Trance Induction

The sound of waves rolling on the shore can help induce a slight trance state in which such spirits can be perceived. Sit quietly by the water and listen.

Fairy Dew

Dew was considered the most sacred water of all by the Druids. Dew is the first exhaled breath of the Earth at dawn. Collect it from a sacred place, if possible. Bottle it and keep it refrigerated, and use it in preparations, made under the light of the moon, to get the sight and for astral travel.

May Dew Beauty Spell

Dew collected early on May Day morning and rubbed on the face will ensure a lovely complexion for the following year. In Edinburgh, people climbed Arthur's Seat to wash their faces in the dew. The *Daily Record* reported in 1934 that more than 200 girls were on the summit. It was also sprinkled on cattle, or ropes soaked in it were hung in the cattle-shed to ensure a plentiful supply of milk. The dew also had many healing properties and was used for goitre, poor sight, and consumption. Sickly children were washed in dew to strengthen them.

Imbolc Dew Spell

At Imbolc take the morning dew and rub it all over the body to benefit the skin.

Paper Ship

Write your wishes on a piece of paper. Fold this into a paper ship and place it on the fast flowing stream to take your wishes to the Water fairies.

Stone and Water Spell for Removing Negativity

Take a smooth river pebble and hold it in your hands. Imagine the ills you wish to be rid of. Concentrate and project them into the stone. Quickly throw the stone into a fast-flowing stream. Walk away without looking back.

Holy Well

Throw a silver coin into a natural well, speaking your desires as you do so. At the Summer Solstice, Spring Equinox, Imbolc, Ostara, Beltane, and Lughnasa, holy wells become empowered with healing energy.

The Tides

When you are working water magick by the sea, take note of the tides and work accordingly. The flow is when the tide is coming in and is the time for magick concerned with beginnings, conception, and so on. High tide is when the tide reaches highest up the beach and is the time for healing and love magick. The ebb is when the tide is receding, and this is the time for purification and banishing. Low tide is the lowest point the sea reaches on the beach that day, and this time is best spent in deep meditation. The highest tide in the month always corresponds with the full moon, and this is the best time for Water fairy contact.

The Voices of the Ocean

Put a shell to your ear and you will hear the murmuring voices of the ocean. Listen with your inner senses, and you may understand the voices of the Otherworld.

Summoning Sea Spirits

Use a conch shell, sounded at dawn or twilight to summon the spirits of the sea to you.

Spell to Bring Sailors Home Safely

Throw water back into the sea three times, saying:

> *"Spirits of the Sea,*
> *I return to you what belongs to you*
> *Return to me what belongs to me."*

Sand Spell

Write your desires in the sand on the beach and let the sea take it to the sea spirits.

EARTH ELEMENTALS

The spirits of earth inhabit the old burial mounds, the caves, and potholes that burrow deep into the earth. The Gnomes are the best known of the Earth Elementals, referred to by Paracelsus as pygmies or *gnomi* who could move through the earth as fish move through water. The word may relate to the Greek verb *gnosis* ("to know") or to *ge-nomos*, which means "earth-dweller." Gnomes have captured the popular imagination as guardians of the earth—particularly the suburban garden—depicted as jolly faced little men wearing red caps.

Dwarfs live in the underground caves, away from the daylight. Early sources do not mention that dwarfs were short in stature, but emphasise that they were great craftsmen and very wise. They possessed stones that gave them immense strength and others that made them invisible. They mine precious stones and metals, guard the Earth and its riches, and are spirits of rocks and caverns, kin to the subterranean Knockers and Mine Fairies that miners must appease. In popular lore, dwarfs live within the Scandinavian and German mountains. They move easily through the earth and are masters of all its minerals.

The earth has many guardian spirits, such as the Icelandic *Landvættir* ("Land Wights"), who protect the land itself and live within the stones, streams, trees, rivers, and features of the landscape. There was a legal requirement that Icelandic long ships had to remove their dragon-head carvings when approaching home to prevent them frightening away the Landvættir. A multitude of Landvættir in various forms chased away a scout of King Harald's invasion fleet. Certain areas were not settled at all, but reserved for the Landvættir. Ceremonies were performed in their honour and offerings left for them.

In addition, Earth fairies include those spirits who inhabit trees, such as dryads, plants devas, vegetation spirits, forest fairies and mountain fairies, green ladies and the woodwoses or wildmen. Woodwoses have a shaggy appearance, often naked and covered only in their own hair. They are connected with the Green Man, who personified the life of the vegetation spirits. In Britain, this spirit of vegetation is still portrayed on May Day by the Green Man, Jack in the Bush, or Jack in the Green, in the guise of a mummer clad in green leaves and fresh boughs. He also occurs on numerous pub signs and church carvings as a head with shoots and leaves growing from the mouth.

The Powers of Earth

What we do to the earth, we do to ourselves because we are connected with it. We have lost our natural ability to contact the Earth spirits, and this can only be regained by recapturng our spiritual contact with nature. From the Earth spirits we learn that we must be rooted in the physical realm; it connects us to who we are, to the past, to our ancestors, to our land. Any plant disconnected from its roots will wither and die.

To connect with the spirits of Earth, look with eyes open to the sacred, rather than the mundane. Try to maintain a feeling of reverence and observation. When Australian aborigines visit a new place they first sing up the land—to greet it and announce their visit in a respectful way. When visiting or working with a new site, you should approach in silence and with deference, demanding nothing—this is not your right. Some places welcome you with open arms and are happy to work with humans on all sorts of levels; other places will permit certain activities but not others. Some may be protected by Elemental spirits and barrow wights that do not welcome human contact and who will cause accidents to drive people away.

The powers of Earth are concerned with what is manifest, the material, the fixed, the solid, the practical, with what is rooted. Earth Elemental magick might be concerned with manifestation, business, health, practicality, wealth, stability, grounding and centring, and agriculture.

People who have a lot of Earth in their psychological make-up are practical, stable, hard-working, dextrous and reliable, determined, patient, logical, and ambitious. However, too much Earth can manifest as laziness, bigotry, gluttony, pedantry, snobbery, clumsiness, stubbornness, and inflexibility.

The Correspondences of Earth

Symbols: stone, mirror, shield, tree, pentacle.

Colours: green, ochre, brown, rust, black.

Direction: north.

Season: winter.

Time: midnight.

Life Tide: death and rebirth.

Magickal Influences: manifestation, practicality, health, wealth, crystals, image magick.

Gems: Green moss agate, emerald, green jasper, jet, malachite, olivine, peridot, green tourmaline, turquoise.

Quality: silence.

Vowel Sound: A.

Sense: touch.

Key Words: darkness, reflection, returning, coldness, winter, rest, peace, practicality, the material world, health, stability, roots, grounding, foundation, permanence, structure, crystallisation, ancestors.

Herbs: cypress, patchouli, vervain, honeysuckle, mugwort, fern, vertivert, primrose, horehound.

Animals: goats, hibernating creatures, dragons, mythical animals.

Earth Elemental Spells and Rituals

To Contact the Earth Spirits

Go out into the countryside at dawn or twilight. Practice the dreaming with the eyes open technique and watch the sun rise or set and the light change. Be aware that the spirit of the landscape changes with it, and power floods in during the "between" times.

To Make an Offering to the Earth Spirits

Take some fresh thyme, rosemary, and white rose petals. Bake them into a cake with oatmeal, milk, and honey, and place it in your garden or special place for fairy contact at the full moon with the words:

> *"I make this offering to honour you,*
> *spirits of this place."*

Fill it with your power, and nurture its growth. Protect it and keep it sacred.

Dowsing a Power Spot

Every place has its own spirit, its own power. Some places will resonate with your own energies, and you will feel stronger when you sit or stand there. You can try this yourself in your own house or garden; use a pendulum to locate it if you like. You probably already do it unconsciously—you may feel more comfortable sitting in one chair than another, and so on. Try performing your meditations and exercises in this spot and feel the difference. Try locating a spot that has an opposite effect—that is one that drains or confuses your energies.

Geomancy

This is a technique of using patterns in sand or in the earth for divination. Take a bowl of sand or fine-sieved earth and rake it smooth. Close your eyes, let your mind drift, and make some marks in the sand with your fingers. When you open your eyes, you will see lines and shapes. Try to interpret them intuitively.

Garden Gnomes

Ceramic gnomes may be considered rather twee, but they represent the protective powers of Earth fairies in the garden.

Three-Stone Oracle

To answer a question, mark a small circle on a piece of paper or board. Pick up a black stone, a white stone, and a grey stone. Ask the spirits of stone to help you answer your question, which must be one with a yes or no answer. Drop the three stones onto the board. If the black stone falls nearest the circle, the answer is *no*. if the white stone is nearest, the answer is *yes*. If the grey stone is nearest, the answer is *wait*.

Image Magick

Image magick falls under the dominion of the Earth Elementals. People often think this is used for cursing—a voodoo doll stuck with pins. In fact, the witch uses a wax image for healing.

Method: Make an image of wax. You don't have to be a great sculptor, but make it recognizably male or female. Incorporate some hair or nails from the person to be healed. A photograph of the face may be stuck on the head of the doll. Go to a place of the Earth Elementals. Put your wand on its chest and name it for the person concerned. Next choose a piece of cloth:

> Red for strength.
>
> Blue for healing.
>
> Yellow to clear the mind.
>
> Orange to heal depression.

Wrap the doll in the chosen cloth and leave it on the altar or other safe place until the healing is completed.

After the aim has been achieved wash the doll in running water. Place your athame on its breast and say:

"You are no longer the image of [such and such]. *Return to the Elements from which you came."*

Break it into pieces and throw it in running water.

Planting the Seed

During a waxing moon when the energies are increasing, plant a seed in a pot as a token of your wish to grow spiritually. Care for it and as it grows, so will you.

Crystal Healing

Take a clear quartz crystal and wash it under running water to rid it of any accrued negativity. Place it in the sunlight for one whole Sunday to charge it with energy. Hold it against your forehead and visualize the purpose for which you wish to use it. You may wish to use it to heal Auntie's rheumatism, or Mother's backache, or your friend's migraines, and so on, but the crystal may only be used for one purpose at a time. When you have the purpose fixed firmly in your mind, "project" it into the crystal. You may then either give the crystal to the person concerned or place it on your altar. The crystal will continue to work for its programmed purpose until you wash and reprogram it.

Agate Friendship Amulet

Wash a piece of agate in running water and anoint it with honeysuckle and patchouli oil. Carry it about your person to attract friends.

Amber and Jet Witch's Necklace

Amber acquires a negative electrical charge when it is rubbed, and was called *elekton* by the ancient Greeks. From this we get our word *electricity*. Amber will carry a magickal charge, and as such forms part of the witches' traditional necklace, along with jet. These should be strung together with the pieces in multiples of three—that is, three amber beads then three jet beads, or six amber and six jet, and so on. As you string them, chant power into them:

"Amber and jet now in this hour.

Amber and jet now feel the power.

Amber and jet now in this hour.

Amber and jet now feel the power."

Continue chanting as you make your necklace.

Amethyst Dream Charm

Wash a piece of amethyst under running water and anoint it with clary sage oil. Place it under your pillow to receive prophetic dreams.

Aventurine-Charged Water for Creativity

To aid visualization and gain inspiration for artists, writers, and generally creative people, leave a piece of green aventurine in water overnight and drink, the next morning, saying:

"Spirits of earth and stone,
Fill me with inspiration.
Aid my vision and creativity,
And I will fashion things in your honour."

Jade Amulet

Jade is especially prized in China as the most magickal stone. Wear a jade bracelet for long life, good health, and to prevent misfortune.

Lodestone Attraction Spell

Carry a lodestone in your pocket to attract new friends. When you are in a social gathering, or when you meet a new person, touch the stone and say:

"Lodestone bring new friends my way,
But lodestone keep my enemies at bay."

Hag Stone Amulet

Search a beach until you find a natural stone with a hole through it. This is called a Hag Stone and is sacred to the Goddess. Take it home and wash it in salt-water saying:

"Gracious spirits I have found
A holy-stone upon the ground.
Some helpful spirit has given me
This token of the One in Three."

Keep it on your altar and, when you take a bath, place the Hag Stone in the water along with a little salt. Feel the warm healing water surrounding you, imbued with the power of the water spirits. When you pull the plug, imagine your illness draining away with the dirty water.

Taking Magickal Plants

If you wish to take wood or herbs from the forest, you must seek the permission of the Green Lady. Mark the plant you want with a piece of thread, then tell the Green Lady why you want its gifts, asking her permission to take it. If you don't think you've had a reply, or are not sure, leave it alone. Only take a little of any one plant, and don't strip it bare so that the plant will die, or the Green Lady will not welcome you back into her domain. Traditionally you should leave her an offering of three handfuls of flax seed.

Ash Tree Healing Wand

The buds of the ash grow in a spiral formation, an ancient symbol of life, growth, and rebirth. Therefore an ash wand can be an important healing tool. Search in spring until you find an "even ash"—that is, an ash tree with an even number of branches on each side. With the proper rituals, cut a branch approximately two feet long saying, "*Sacred ash, sacred ash, give this wand to me.*" Pass the branch though a candle flame, sprinkle with water, pass it through the air, and then touch it to the earth and say:

"Through Fire, Water, Air, and Earth,
I consecrate this wand in the names
of the spirits of the Elements."

Use the wand to channel healing power.

Traditional Oak Healing Spell

For aches and pains take a handful of oak leaves and a piece of red carnelian and sew them into a muslin bag. Rub it over the affected parts then go at dawn to an oak tree and place the muslin bag into a hollow on the east side of the tree saying:

"Oaken tree, oaken tree,
Take these pains from me."

Stop the hole with oak bark and walk away without looking back.

Apple Tree Healing Spell

Red thread 24 inches long

White thread 24 inches long

Black thread 24 inches long

Method: If you are lucky enough to have an apple tree in your garden or local park, you can perform this healing spell. Braid the red, white, and black threads together while thinking about the illness you want to be rid of. Visualize braiding it into the threads. Go out into the garden and, using your right hand, tie your left hand to an apple tree with the thread. Be sure to leave a loose loop. Slip your hand out of the loop and walk home without looking behind you, being aware of leaving the disease behind. The apple tree will transmit the negativity into the earth, where Mother Earth will absorb and transform it.

AIR ELEMENTALS

Sylphs are spirits of the Air and usually live high in the mountain peaks. Sometimes their voices are heard on the wind or their airy forms are felt in passing, though they are rarely seen. They are described as almost transparent, very small, and winged, or, alternatively, as tall with long feathered wings, large, hawk-like eyes, and angular faces.

The term *Sylph* is derived from the Greek word *silphe*, which means a "butterfly" or "moth"—indeed, fairies are popularly depicted with butterfly wings. The ancient Celts regarded butterflies as symbols of fairies or ancestral spirits (often considered as one and the same), and they appear in Celtic stories as guides to the Otherworld or Fairyland, where the dead also dwelt. Ariel is the king of Air Elementals and controls all the powers of air. His winds circle the Earth. Shakespeare mentioned him in *The Tempest*, saying that, with his song, he could bind or loosen the winds, enchant men or drive them mad.

In popular lore Zephyrs are the guardians of the winds. In Greek myth, Zephyr was the west wind, son of Aurora, goddess of dawn. He was the lover of Flora, goddess of flowers, and together they cause the flowers to grow in spring.

Some fairies seem to represent spirits of weather, particularly whirlwinds, wind, storm, rain, lightning, sunshine, and so on. The Wind Knots or Folletti of Italy ride storms, the Guriuz bring good weather to farmers, Munya is the lightning while her brothers are the two thunders, the Salvanelli raise storms to ride on the wind and the Swedish Skosrå is a violent whirlwind. The Innuits believed in an important air spirit, one of the three primary spirits along with the moon and sea. Known as Sila ("Weather" or "Intelligence"), the spirit lived far above the earth and controlled the weather, but punished human misdeeds with sickness and bad weather.

The Powers of Air

Air spirits are concerned with the spiritual life, freedom, and purity. "Spirit" is derived from *spiro*, "I breathe." "Wind" and "breath" and "spirit" were believed by many peoples to be identical. In Egyptian mythology, the god Khnûmû, or Knef (the Kneph of the Greeks), was a wind god. *Knef* means "wind," "breath," and "spirit" or "the air of life." In Memphis, the chief god was Her-shef, who breathed from his nostrils the north wind, which gave life to every living being.

Breath is a divine gift, returned to the giver at death. The secret of breath is part of the magick of air. We take air into us that contains vital energy that some call *prana* and others *chi*. When we breathe in deeply, we inhale this life force and rhythmic breathing exercises help to attune you to the powers of Air.

Inhaled air is the sustaining breath of life; exhaled air carries the words, poetry, and song that communicate human ideas and knowledge. In many myths, creation is brought to life when a god breathes into it. It was often thought that spirit could be blown into or out of people. Demons were also blown out of people.

The powers of Air are also concerned with the intellect, the powers of the mind, knowledge (as opposed to wisdom), logic, inspiration, information, teaching, memory, thought, and communication. Like the other Elements, the powers of Air can be constructive or destructive. The gentle breeze cools and brings the life giving rain, but it can become the destructive hurricane. It is for this reason that the magickal symbol of Air is a double-edged sword.

The voice of the Air spirits is heard in the wind. There were many scared groves where the voices of spirits were heard in the wind whispering in the trees. The head of the alder was used as whistle so that the spirits might speak through it. The druids were attuned to interpreting these voices, and *druid* means "oak knowledge."

People who have Air dominant in their psychological make-up are flexible, versatile, dextrous, tasteful, idealistic, original, individual, and tolerant. However, they can also be distant, opinionated, easily bored, impatient, self-deceiving, superficial, indecisive, quarrelsome, manipulative, thoughtless, cruel, fickle, inconsistent, unreliable, and two-faced.

The Correspondences of Air

Symbols: athame, sword, arrow, feather, egg.

Colours: yellow, silver, gold.

Direction: east.

Season: spring.

Time: dawn.

Life Tide: youth.

Magickal Influences: the non-tangible affecting the tangible, psychism, mental ability, protection, prophecy, visualization.

Gems: topaz, aventurine, mica, fluorite, citrine.

Quality: the mind, thought.

Vowel Sound: E.

Sense: hearing.

Key Words: wind, movement, inception, emergence, flying, sound, germination, inspiration, planning, communication, ideas, understanding, awareness, memory, mind, intelligence, knowledge.

Herbs: lavender, lemongrass, verbena, marjoram, mint, acacia, almond, benzoin, gum mastic.

Animals: butterflies, eagle, hawk, and birds.

Air Elemental Spells and Rituals

To Encounter an Air Elemental

3 grains frankincense

3 hawk feathers

3 mint leaves

3 topaz stones

9-inch square yellow silk

1 yard yellow silk thread

Method: Wrap the ingredients in the yellow silk and tie with the yellow thread. Take the parcel to a windswept three-way crossroads and say:

> *"Powerful sylphs, spirits of Air,*
> *Accept this gift as my offering to you.*
> *Make yourself known to me*
> *And aid me in my work."*
> (State your wish.)

Winds of Change

Fill three glass balls with mint, lemon grass, lavender flowers, acacia resin, and marjoram while asking the powers of Air to blow the winds of change through your life. Hang in the trees of your garden where the winds can blow them.

Message on the Wind

Hold a feather (any real feather will do) in your hand and think hard about the message you wish to send, visualising the person you wish to send it to. Tie this onto a tree so that the wind can blow it, saying:

> *"Spirits of the Air,*
> *Spirits of the Air,*
> *Carry this message for me,*

Blown on the wind,
Carried on your breath.
Carry this message for me,
Spirits of Air,
And I will pour you a libation of
sweet, white milk."

Breathing Out Pain

When you are troubled by pain, visualise the part of the body that hurts, breathe in, and imagine breathing out through the part of the body in pain. Do this for several minutes and you will find the pain easing. This really works!

Kite Divination

Take a yellow kite and anoint its spars with rosemary oil. Fly the kite and let the wind play with it. Ask a question. If the kite bobs up and down, the answer is *yes*.

North Wind Spell

When the wind is blowing from the north, you can use its power to dispel negativity or illness. Go to a hill, write the problem on a piece of paper, tear the paper into tiny pieces, and let the wind blow them away.

East Wind Spell

A handful of seed corn
1 whole egg
3 feathers

Method: On a windy hill at sunrise, say:

> *"Spirits of the East Wind,*
> *Accept this offering from me:*
> *Seed for new beginnings,*
> *Egg for potential,*
> *Feathers for your powers.*
> *Help me make a new beginning,*
> *And change my life and luck for the better."*

Bury the corn and egg, and allow the wind to take the feathers.

South Wind Spell

The south wind is a hot, firy wind, filled with power, energy, and excitement. When the south wind blows, go to a windy place and light a candle in a lantern or glass jar and say:

> *"Spirit of the South wind,*
> *That brings the fiery heat*
> *Bring passion and excitement into my life*
> *And fill me with your energy."*

West Wind Spell

When the west wind blows, go to a windy place near a body of water, take some crystal water or morning dew, and sprinkle it into the west wind, saying:

> *"Spirit of the west wind*
> *That brings the gentle rain,*
> *Purify me and cleanse me of all negativity,*
> *Bring love and friendship into my life,*
> *And bless me with your gentle warmth."*

Wind Chime Spell

Hang up a wind chime to call love to you with these words:

> *"As you chime in the breeze,*
> *Let the call of love go out on the wind,*
> *And bring my lover to my door."*

To Bind the Wind

The old witches would tie the winds up with a length of rope, pulling the knots tight to tie up the storm, and releasing them when the wind is required. Undoing the first knot would give a light breeze, the second a strong wind, and the third a gale.

To Still the Wind

Tie four feathers together and bury them beneath a bowl of salt.

Bull Roarer

To call the spirits of Air, take a piece of wood and tie it onto a leather thong. Whirl this around your head until it makes a high-pitched sound. This is called a bull roarer. You may have to experiment a little with the shape of the wood.

Wind Chime Remembrance Spell

This idea comes from a friend who runs an animal sanctuary. When her animals die, she inscribes their names on the tubes of wind chimes, and when the chimes blow about and sound in the wind, the animals are remembered.

Dispelling Bells

In magick, the sound of bells is often used to dispel negativity. Hang a line of small bells in your garden to put it under the protection of the Air fairies, and, as the bells sound, all ill will will be driven away.

Hag Stone Charm

To ensure a favourable breeze for sailing, pour milk, ale, or honey into a hag stone.

FIRE ELEMENTALS

As well as the many house fairies that live in the hearth or behind the stove, there are spirits that represent the Fire itself. In Northern European countries, they were called drakes, salamanders, or dragons. They are said smell like rotten eggs, and their presence is usually only betrayed by the stench, though they are sometimes glimpsed as a flaming ball. They only take on the character of fire when they fly, when they look like streaks of flame or fiery balls with long tails. Otherwise they look like small boys with red caps and coats. Some are house fairies who move into a house and keep the firewood dry and bring gifts of gold and grain to the master of the house. The bond is between the male head of the house and the male drake, and is a serious pact, often written in blood. The drake takes care of the house, barn, and stables, making sure that the pantry and money chest are well stocked. They can travel the world in a split second and bring their masters a present back from far away places. In return, the master keeps the drake fed and treated with respect.

Should the drake be insulted the house will not be there long. If you see a drake on its travels, take shelter, for they leave behind a poisonous sulphurous fug. If you quickly shout "half and half," or throw a knife at the creature, then the drake may drop some of its booty in your lap. If two people together see a drake, they should cross their legs in silence, take the fourth wheel off the wagon and take shelter. The drake will then be compelled to leave them some of his haul.

The spirit of the hearth fire is often thought of as female and was once widely worshipped as a goddess. In Greek myth she was Hestia. Her name, according to Plato, means "the essence of things," a formless essence symbolized by the flame, which flows through everything that has life. As the domestic hearth is the sacred centre of the home, the hearth of the gods is the centre of the cosmos. She presided over all hearth and altar fires, and she was worshipped every day with prayers offered to her before and after meals. Hearth was in the care of the woman of the home and before each meal something was thrown on the fire as an offering.

In Celtic lore, the spirit of the hearth is Brighid. She was invited into the home by the woman of the house, in the form of a doll or corn dolly dressed in maiden white. Oracles were taken from the ashes of the hearth fire, which people examined for a sign that Brighid had visited—that is, a mark that looked like a swan's footprint. If found, it was a lucky omen (the swan was an ancient attribute of the goddess Brighid). Many Irish homes still have a Brighid's cross hung up. This four equal-armed cross was originally a solar symbol as Bridhid is a goddess of Fire and Sun.

There are many other Fire spirits. The Arabian Djinn, for example, are composed of fire without smoke, with fire in their veins instead of blood. Will o' the Wisps are bog fairies that appear as curious lights, usually seen flickering in the distance over swamps and marshes. They jump and dance along with the aim of leading travellers astray. Perhaps the most common name is Jack-a-lantern or Jack O'Lantern. In Wales the Will o' the Wisp is called *ellylldan* meaning "Fire fairy." It can be seen dancing about on marshy ground, into which it may lead a hapless traveller. When the Will o' the Wisp appears at sea it is generally called St Elmo's Fire, and is seen on ship's masts and accompanied by a crackling sound.

There is a connection between trades that use fire and magick. The supernatural reputation of the smith persisted in Europe into the 19th century and is still extant in India and Africa. In Britain, it was believed that smiths were blood charmers (healers) and could foretell the future. Even the water the smith used to cool metal had magickal properties and was much sought after for healing purposes. A smithy-forged nail, hammered into a tree, was thought to transfer the illness to the tree. Smiths also possessed the secret of the Horseman's Word, which, when whispered into the ear of the wildest horse, would calm it. People swore oaths by the smith's anvil, and in some places he had the authority to marry couples, as at the famous Gretna Green in Scotland. In fairy stories, smiths often protect people and animals against malignant fairies, evil spirits, witchcraft, and the evil eye.

The Powers of Fire

Fire is the most mysterious of all the Elements. It seems almost supernatural in comparison to Earth, Air, or Water. The spirits of Fire are concerned with creativity, life energy, and the spirit. Fire generates illumination within the light of the spirit. Fire gives us the power of energy, igniting action, animation, and movement. It sparks courage and acts of bravery. It heats passion and enthusiasm. Fire is the power of inner sight and creative vision, directing it and controlling it to make it manifest in the world, the dominion of Will. It is the glow of the candle flame, the warmth of the hearth, the burning heat of the desert, the incandescence of the sun. However, fire transforms what it consumes, a power that may either purify or destroy. Fire is wild, untameable, and dangerous; it can burn those around it. This is true of the Fire spirits, too. They are intense and impatient of human ignorance; they can be intolerant of our failings, and capable of infernos of rage and intemperance.

Rituals connected with Fire spirits are necessarily concerned with placating the spirits, availing ourselves of their gifts while averting disaster. A friend of mine invented a divination system she called Ken Sticks. *Ken* is a rune connected with illumination and fire. She used nine matches, invoking the powers of Ken into each as the match was struck and flared, then blown out. The matches were then thrown onto a cloth and the resulting rune shapes of the fallen matches read. Shortly after inventing this method, she taught it at a workshop to nine people. Thus there were nine times nine invocations of

Ken—fire. After the workshop we stayed at a hotel that caught fire twice in the same night. Other workshop attendees also experienced unexplained outbreaks of fire. Fortunately, no one was hurt, but be warned!

Fire is an agent of transformation: The food in the cauldron is changed as it cooks, raw ores and metals are altered into useful objects on the blacksmith's forge, and it alters the materials it consumes into ashes. Fairies and other spirits were attracted by these fires and circled round them, and sometimes had to be placated so that they would not cause trouble and steal the feast. Fire spirits are agents of cleansing. Cattle were driven over the ashes of the Beltane and Samhain fires to purify them, and flaming torches were carried around the crops at Midsummer to protect them.

Fire symbolizes the life force. It was associated with the fertility of the land, and the ashes of the sacred fires were scattered on the land, to transfer the vigour of the Fire spirits into the Earth. It was also connected with the fertility of humans. Young men would leap through the festival fires to increase their virility, and young women jumped to become fertile. Fire magick is concerned with action and will. Fire corresponds to energy, power, passion, vitality.

People with a preponderance of Fire in their make-up are energetic, vital, passionate, creative, intuitive, generous, courageous, driven, friendly, enterprising, philanthropic, warm, cheerful, and honourable. However, they can also be ostentatious, arrogant, excessive, dominating, vain, promiscuous, aggressive, tactless, and opinionated.

The Correspondences of Fire

Symbols: wand, staff, candles, torches.

Colours: red, orange, flame, gold.

Direction: south.

Season: summer.

Time: noon.

Life Tide: maturity.

Magickal Influences: active energy, illumination, wisdom, willpower, passion, healing.

Gems: red agate, amber, bloodstone, carnelian, citrine, quartz, diamond, garnet, red jasper, lava, ruby, sard, sardonyx, sunstone, topaz, red tourmaline.

Quality: directing.

Vowel Sound: I.

Sense: smell.

Key Words: burning, light, flame, energy, growth, balancing, directing, controlling, illuminating, transforming, passion, fertility, virility, courage, lust, force, enthusiasm, desire, energy, courage, initiative, creativity, dynamism, radiance, illumination.

Herbs: allspice, frankincense, ginger, juniper, marigold, orange, rosemary, dragon's blood, clove, bay, ash.

Animals: lions, lizards, salamanders.

Fire Elemental Spells and Rituals

Household Spirits Shrine

For the ancients, the hearth-place was also the altar of the household spirits, where offerings could be made; when you being to think of your home as having indwelling spirit it can make a huge difference to the quality of life within it. You can use your mantelpiece as an altar, and many people do, or you can make a small shrine or niche beside it. What you put on that altar is up to you. You might want statues of gods and goddesses or a fairy to represent the house spirit. You could bring the outside in by adding stones, crystals, or leaves, plus candles and your magickal tools if this seems appropriate. Change the flowers often and decorate it for the Eight Festivals. As the place of protection, decorate it with shiny horse brasses, which attract sun energy and deflect negativity.

Hearth Spirit Shrine

As well as protective ancestral spirits, the spirit of hearth and Fire dwells within every hearth, whether large or small. In many ancient religions, a fire was kept constantly burning to represent the presence of the divine. Nowadays, you probably don't have a fire in your home all the time, if at all. But you can celebrate the living flame with candles, joss sticks, incense on charcoal, and oil lamps.

The Hearth as Cosmic Axis

As the dwelling place of the living flame, the hearth was a holy place, a threshold between this world and the realm of the gods. Its rising smoke took prayers to the gods of the Upperworld; the gods of the Worlds Below could be contacted through the hearthstone. Offerings were placed on the hearthstone. In many tales, the hearth and chimney are the entrance and egress of spirits. In lore, various fairies are said to live behind the hearth or to come down the chimney.

Bonfire Spell

If you wish to be rid of something, a bad habit or a painful situation for example, write it on a piece of paper and throw it onto the bonfire and watch it burn away.

Candle Magick

Decide what spell you wish to work and choose a candle in the appropriate colour.

Colour	Perfume	Basic Energy
Black	Cypress	endings
Blue	Camomile	healing, protection
Gold	Juniper	spiritual strength
Green	Patchouli	fertility, growth, creativity
Indigo	clary sage	vision
Orange	Melissa	optimism, success, bravery
Pink	Rose	love
Purple	Thyme	strength, mastery
Red	Ginger	life, vitality, energy, sex drive
Silver	Lemon	intuition, truth, enlightenment
Violet	Lavender	spiritual growth
White	Frankincense	purity, cleansing
Yellow	Rosemary	intellectual development, strength of mind

Method: Set it up on a low table one evening and put out most of the lights in the room. Take the corresponding oil and anoint the candle middle to top and middle to bottom with the oil, concentrating on what you want to achieve. When you are satisfied, light the candle, saying:

"By this candle's burning light,
Sending magick into the night,
By my will the spell be done,
By this act my wish be won,
By the Goddess, the one in three,
As I will so mote it be."

Leave it to burn itself out. (Make sure it is in a safe place.)

Only perform the operation for this particular purpose *once* in any 12-month period, and only perform it when you want a change in the course of events, *not* when you want to enhance something that is already happening, or if you want something to remain the same. Don't expect things to happen immediately; it may take time to work itself out.

Birthday Candles

Blowing the candles out on a birthday cakes symbolizes life continuing beyond the extinguished years.

Healing-Sun Charm Bag

This charm calls upon the power of the Sun for healing. You will need:

> 6-inch circle of yellow cloth or yellow charm bag
>
> Gold thread
>
> 2 tsp. bay leaves
>
> 2 tsp. chamomile flowers
>
> Pinch cinnamon powder
>
> 2 tsp. marigold petals
>
> 2 tsp. rosemary leaves
>
> Piece of amber

Method: Lay out the cloth and place the amber in the centre of it, then sprinkle on the herbs saying:

> *"Golden spirit of the Sun and healing,*
> *I call upon you to lend me your power*
> *And bless this healing charm.*
> *Imbue it with your strength and energy*
> *So that it shall heal and restore me.*
> *Blessed Be."*

Tie up the bag with the gold thread and keep it near you.

Energizing Sun Oil

> 30 ml sunflower oil
>
> 5 drops orange essential oil

5 drops lemon essential oil

2 drops lime essential oil

5 drops rosemary essential oil

Method: Pour the sunflower oil into a dark glass bottle and add the drops of essential oil. Keep tightly stoppered. This blend contains some powerful plant oils that will give a boost to your physical energy levels. When you feel in need of extra energy you can rub a little of the oil on your arms and neck, pour a little in your bath, evaporate some in an oil burner, or simply sniff the bottle. (**Note:** Some people may be allergic to certain oils. Please take advice from a qualified therapist before use.)

Crystal Ball Healing

If you have a crystal ball (a clear glass or quartz sphere) then you can use it in a healing spell; the ball represents wholeness and perfection, and the aim of the spell is to draw the healing power of the Sun into the body through the ball. On a sunny day go outside and move the ball about until the sun's rays are concentrated through it onto the affected part of the body. Say:

"Lord of Sun and Lord of Day,
Who lights the world upon its way,
Turn your gaze and see my pain,

Channel health and strength again
Through this sphere—I feel your power
Making me whole and new this hour."

Rub the affected part with the ball.

Fire Smooring Ritual

At night the fire should be covered in a special way to appease the hearth spirit. The embers are divided into three equal sections, with a peat laid between each section, each one touching a little mound in the middle. The first peat is laid down in the name of the spirit of Life, the second in the name of the spirit of Peace, and the third in the name of the spirit of Grace. The woman of the house then covers the circle with ashes, a process known as *smooring*, taking care not to put out the fire, in the name of the Three of Light [originally the goddess Brighid]. A protective prayer is then said over it:

"Protect my house and family.
Keep my hearth warm and
welcoming to all who come,
In the name of the Three of Light."

Moving House Ritual

When moving to a new house it was often the custom to take live coals from the previous one to ensure the continuation of the life and spirit of the home and family. You can repeat a similar custom by lighting a candle brought from your old home into the new one. This echoes the carrying of Hestia's sacred fire to new colonies and towns.

Pyromancy

Lamps and fires were kept in temples not just to illuminate the place, but to embody the living spirit of Fire. When our ancestors danced around the flames, they were dancing around vital spirits of Fire. It was believed that these Elementals could speak through the actions of the leaping flames. This is called *pyromancy*, and is a form of divination.

❋ When a fire burns all on one side, or falls into two heaps in the grate, it foretells a parting of some kind.

❋ If it will not start in the morning it predicts quarrels in the house, and arguments are also presaged by a spluttering piece of coal.

❋ A coffin-shaped piece of coal flying out of the fire and into the room foreshadows a death.

❋ A cradle-shaped piece of coal means a birth.

❋ A cluster of bright sparks at the back of the chimney means good news on the way,

❋ Dull sparks mean bad news.

❋ Showers of gold sparks indicate money.

❋ Blue flames in the fire indicate coming frosts.

Nyd Fire

The Nyd Fire, or Need Fire, is a sacred fire lit on magickal occasions or fairy festivals by using friction or light projected by a magnifying glass.

Conclusion

mazingly similar stories of fairies, under a variety of names, exist around the world from Africa to the Americas: They are white and shining, they can appear in animal form, they live in the underworld with the dead or in an Otherworldly paradise; they are responsible both for the fertility of the land, and can also cause disease, blight, decay, and death. Wherever we find fairies in the world (and they are everywhere), their names, more often than not, simply mean "spirit" or else "shining" and sometimes just "lord" or "lady."

In these legends of fairies, we can trace pre-Christian concepts of nature spirits, along with the principles of dealing with them. Even into the 19th and early 20th centuries, the good Christian farmers of Europe believed in spirits of land and water that could affect the growth of the crops and the fecundity of the land itself. There is plenty of evidence in Britain, Ireland, and the rest of Western Europe that regular offerings were made to the fairies, on stones in the corners of fields, on the hearth, and in special places outside the farmhouse door. These offerings were to placate them, to prevent them doing harm, and to win their help and friendship.

Fairies could make the crops bountiful and animals hale and hearty, and they protected their favourite humans from harm, occasionally gave them great riches, beauty, or magical powers. They could bestow the power to heal or give a person the ability to make wonderful music or beautiful works of art and craftsmanship.

219

The idea that fairies could also be harmful beings—if they chose—was universal, but one that is divorced from the concepts of tiny cute Tinkerbells that are entirely modern and have their roots in bowdlerized Victorian nursery tales, not real fairy lore. Fairies could blight the crops, make fields and animals barren, and steal the goodness from food. Fairies could also steal the spirit of the land itself; the fields appeared to yield a crop but the ears of corn would not fill out, the harvest would be slender and the animal fodder without nourishment. Fairies were thought to use elf bolts to cause harm, propelling them into humans or livestock. Deaths were attributed to them and it was thought they could induce paralysisand other illnesses, such as blisters, cramps, tuberculosis, rheumatism, and bruising in return for offending the fairies.

Fairies also took the souls of animals and humans away to Fairyland. If a child became ill it was suspected of being a changeling, a fairy child substituted for a human one. So strong was that belief in rural Ireland, that in 1895 Brigit Cleary was burned to death under suspicion of being a changeling. When Bridget had failed to recover from an illness, her family decided that she must be possessed by a malevolent fairy and tried to expel it with doses of urine and herbs. When this failed her loving family resorted to the purification of fire.

It was necessary to take precautions against the powerful and easily offended fairies. It was considered politic to keep most of them out of the house by putting protective patterns on the hearth and threshold. The water in which feet had been washed gave them access, so this was carefully disposed of. Iron horseshoes were hung over the door to prevent their entrance. Children were protected with iron charms and red thread, and iron nails were carried in the pocket when travelling.

When things went wrong, or relationships with the fairies broke down completely, it was necessary to call in an expert: the wise woman, cunning man, or fairy doctor. These were people with special gifts, who knew how to see fairies, how to travel into their realm, and who gained their knowledge from the fairies themselves. Evidence of the continuity of these beliefs in Europe, and accounts of many such practitioners, is readily traceable from the Dark Ages onward, through the 1960s and beyond.

In the practices and taboos surrounding fairies, there are many parallels with shamanic cultures. These include working with animal totems and familiar spirits, the feeding of the familiars, travels to the otherworld, the association of the spirits of the Otherworld with the ancestors and the spirits of the dead, and the various offerings made to the spirits. Nor were these beliefs confined to the witches and cunning men, but shared by the general population, even the most learned and distinguished, as evidenced by the writings of King James I. It is in these beliefs and traditions that we find the real roots of modern witchcraft.

Chapter
Notes

Chapter 1

1. Institute of Ethnology and Folk-lore Research 2004, *www.ief.hr*.
2. Quoted in Brian Bates, *The Real Middle Earth*, p. 107.
3. Quoted in Brian Bates, *The Real Middle Earth.*

Chapter 2

1. Nigel Pennick personal communication.
2. Nigel Pennick, "Spirits of the Landscape," *Silver Wheel Magazine*, Beltane 2005.
3. Graves, Robert, *The White Goddess*, Faber and Faber, 1961.

Chapter 4

1. W.B.Yeats, *Folk and Fairy Tales of the Irish Peasantry,* 1888.

Chapter 5

1. Claire O'Rush, *The Enchanted Garden,* Blandford, London, 1996.

Chapter 6

1. *The Witch's Familiar and the Fairy in Early Modern England and Scotland Folk-lore,* Oct. 2000, by Emma Wilby.
2. W.B.Yeats, *Folk and Fairy Tales of the Irish Peasantry, 1888.*
3. W.C.Hazlitt, *The Romance of King Orfeo,* London, 1875.
4. W. Bottrell, *Traditions and Hearthside Stories of the West of Cornwall,* Penzance, 1870.
5. Nigel Pennick, "Spirits of the Landscape," *Silver Wheel Magazine,* Beltane 2005.

Chapter 7

1. Lady Wilde, *Ancient Legends, Mystic Charms and Superstitions of Ireland,* Ward & Downey, London, 1887.
2. Crofton Croker, *Fairy Legends and Traditions of the South of Ireland,* John Murray, London, 1828.

Chapter 8

1. Paracelsus [1493-1541], *Liber de nymphis, sylphis, pygmaeis et salamandris et caeteribus spiritibus.*

Glossary

Aegir: the Norse sea god.

Aelf: the fairies in Scandinavian and Gemanic lore, a word rendered into English as *elf*.

Aine: an Irish fairy woman, originally a goddess, who lives in the mound called Cnoc Aine.

Alfred Watkins (1921): an English brewer who formulated the idea of ley lines linking sacred sites across the country.

Alvgest ("elf wind"): thought to be the breath of elves, which covers the body of a person with blisters

Amenti: an Egyptian goddess associated with the underworld.

Anu: the mother of the Irish fairies, previously a goddess of earth and fertility.

Aradia: many Italian witches believed in the historical existence of a woman (or goddess) named Aradia, who brought about a revival of Italian witchcraft, travelling the country and preaching the old Pagan religion of Diana, whom they called Queen of the Fairies.

Àràk: a Cambodian house fairy who adopts a family and then either dwells in the house with them or in a nearby tree.

Ariadne: daughter of King Minos of Crete, who helped her lover, the hero Theseus, find his way into the labyrinth by giving him a clew (a ball of thread).

Attilio: an Italian house fairy who lives near the hearth and may be a latter-day version of the ancient Roman *lare* or protective household spirit.

Auki: a Peruvian mountain fairy that helps shamans with healing.

Avalon ("Isle of Apples"): a fairy island in British fairy lore.

Bajang: a Malayan spirit or fairy that can be kept as a familiar by a magician who feeds it on eggs and milk.

Banshees: wailing Celtic fairies whose appearance heralds a death in the house.

Bargees: the workers who sail the barges or boats on canals.

Bean-Nighe: a type of banshee that haunts the streams of Scotland and Ireland, washing the bloodstained clothes of those about to die.

Befana: an Italian fairy who appears on Twelfth Night to leave gifts.

Beltane: The Celtic festival marking May Day.

Berchte ("bright one"): a fairy that destroys any spinning left unfinished.

Bifrost: in Norse myth, the rainbow bridge to the Otherworld.

Black Annis: a hag fairy, originally a goddess, of Leicester in England.

Black Dogs: Otherworldly dogs whose appearance is a bad omen.

Blodeuwedd: A Welsh fairy, originally a goddess, who was formed from nine types of flowers.

Bóann: an Irish goddess of the Rover Boyne.

Bon Garçons ("Good Boys"): mischievous French fairies.

Brighid or **Brigit:** an Irish triple goddess of fire.

Brownie: a British house fairy who does household chores in return for a saucer of milk.

Cailleach Bheur ("Blue Hag"): a Scottish hag fairy who ushers in the winter.

Callicantzaroi: Greek fairies that gather to celebrate the Winter Solstice, staring at the sun and vanishing on Twelfth Night.

Ceaird Chomuinn ("Association Craft"): a gift of master craftsmanship that can be bestowed by fairies on those they like.

Centaurs: creatures from Greek myth, half-man, half-horse.

Chakras: In Eastern philosophy, the energy centres of the body.

Chi: in far Eastern philosophy, a type of cosmic energy that permeates all things.

Chimke: a little German house fairy who helps around the house in return for a bowl of milk each night.

Cluricauns: Irish fairies who steal from wine cellars.

Cosmic Axis: an imaginary axis that links all the dimensions of the cosmos.

Cunning Man: in British folklore, a man who deals with the Otherworld, locates lost objects, heals and removes curses.

Danu: a Celtic goddess, the mother of the Tuatha Dé Danaan, which literally translates as "the People of the Goddess Danu."

Daoine Sidhe: Irish fairies of the west or Connacht.

Duduška Domovoy ("Grandfather House Spirit"): is a Russian house fairy who appears as an old man covered in hair, often in the likeness of a family patriarch.

Demeter: in Greek myth, the goddess of the harvest, particularly the grain harvest.

Devas: Fairies that help plants to grow. Every plant, flower, or vegetable has its own Deva.

Diana: In Roman myth, the goddess of the moon. She is associated with both witches and fairies, and her name appears as part of many fairy designations across Europe.

Dinsele ("They Themselves"): Rumanian vampiric fairies that look like large cats walking on two legs.

Dísir (Idis in Anglo-Saxon): Nordic female ancestral spirits who were honoured as a guardian of whichever person, family, or clan that lived on her territory.

Disma ("The Little Ones"): small fairies from Gotland who wear grey or blue clothes and caps upon their heads.

Divna ("the divine"): Serbian fairies that were originally Pagan goddesses, later associated with witch lore.

Djinn: Arabian fairies that have fire in the veins instead of blood.

Dobby: The name for fairies in parts of Northern England.

Domoviyr: Russian fairies that shed their skins in spring and grow lighter ones for the summer.

Drakes: In England, these are fire spirits.

Dryads: In Greek myth, the spirits of individual trees. The dryad can leave her tree to dance, but if the tree is cut down, she will die.

Duende: Spanish house fairies that perform household chores in return for a small reward.

Dwarfs: Earth fairies of the Scandinavian and German mountains. They move easily through the earth and are masters of all its minerals.

Elder Mother or **Elder Queen:** In England,

the fairy spirit of the elder tree. She lived at its roots and was the mother of the elves.

Elen: A Welsh deity, patroness of roads and pathways, including those into the Otherworld.

Ellylldan ("fire fairy"): the Welsh term for a Will o'the Wisp.

Ellyllon: Welsh and Cornish fairies that closely resemble English elves.

Elphame: the Scottish term for Fairyland or the Otherworld.

Epona ("Pony"): a Celtic shamanic goddess that carries a key that unlocks both the stable door and the gates of the Otherworld.

Fachan: a Scots Highland fairy that has one eye, one hand, one leg, one ear, one arm, and one toe all lined up down the centre of his body.

Fairy Godmothers: fairies that appear, usually in triads, at the birth of a child to predict its future or bestow gifts upon it.

Fatae: The Italian word for fairies, derived from the ancient fate goddesses who spin the life thread, measure it, and finally cut it.

Father Christmas: In Britain, the fairy who appears on Christmas Eve, bringing presents for good children.

Father Time: the spirit of the old year, probably derived from the Greek god of time, Cronos.

Fili ("weaver of spells"): an Irish bard.

Finvarra ("White-topped"): an Irish fairy king, originally a god of the underworld.

Fireplace Folletti: Italian fairies who live in the hearth and fix young brides with their hypnotic stares, making them dissatisfied and dispirited.

Follets: bad-tempered French house fairies.

Frau Holda: a German hag fairy who brings the snow in winter by shaking out her feather bed in the sky.

Fridean: Scottish fairies that guard the roads.

Fylgia: in Old Norse, a guardian spirit.

Genius Locus: the guardian spirit or soul of a specific place.

The Gentry: a flattering term for the fairies, who don't like to be called "fairies."

Glamour: a spell that makes one thing seem to be another.

Goblins: unpleasant, ugly fairies that appear in graveyards and other insalubrious places.

The Good Neighbours: a flattering term for the fairies, who don't like to be called "fairies."

Green Ladies: in England, female fairies that dwell in trees.

Green Man: the spirit of vegetation.

Guriuz: bring good weather to farmers.

Gwrach y Rhibyn ("Hag of the Dribble"): a welsh banshee who appears to those with relatives about to die and shrieks their names.

Gwragedd Annwn: female Welsh fairies that dwell beneath the lakes.

Gwyn ap Nudd: a Welsh fairy king who rules the Tylwyth Teg.

Habetrot: a Scottish spinning and weaving fairy.

Hausmänner: a German house fairy.

Hecate: in Greek myth, the goddess of witches.

Herne the Hunter: a wild huntsman in English folklore.

Herodias: a European witch goddess and fairy queen.

Hulda: Nordic Queen of the Dwarfs or the patroness of the elder tree.

Igosha: a Russian house fairy.

Imbolc: an old Celtic festival that marked the first stirrings of spring, on 1st February.

Jack O'Lantern: an English bog or marsh fairy, similar to a Will o'the Wisp.

Jack Robinson: a mischievous English fairy, possibly synonymous with Robin Goodfellow.

Jimaninos: Mexican fairies who dance at the Festival of the Dead.

Jubuk: an Icelandic fairy that visits houses at Christmas. If he is well fed, he will leave without causing any harm, but if not he will spill the beer in the cellar and make the stored grain rot.

Julenisse ("Yule Fairy"): a Norwegian or Danish fairy that delivers Christmas gifts. He looks like a little old man in red clothes.

Ken: the fire rune.

Kindly Ones: a flattering name for the fairies or for the Fates.

Knef or **Kneph:** an Egyptian wind god.

Kodin-HaltiaL: a Finnish house fairy.

Kornbocke: a German fairy who guards the grain and causes it to ripen, riding on the breezes that ripple the cornfields.

Korred: Breton fairies that guard the ancient dolmens and the treasures that lie beneath them.

Kris Kringle: A German fairy that delivers Christmas presents.

Landvættir ("Land Wights"): Icelandic protective spirits or nature fairies that live within the stones, streams, trees, rivers, and features of the landscape.

Lar familiaris ("household lar"): ancient Roman household spirits that were given daily offerings of food and monthly gifts of garlands, all placed on the hearth shrine.

Lares Compitales: ancient Roman spirits that guarded boundaries (a *compita* is the marker of a boundary).

Leanan Sidhe ("fairy sweetheart") or *leannan sith*: a Celtic fairy, of either sex, who seeks the love of mortals.

Les Petits Faîtiaux: Channel Island fairies that live in the old burial mounds and hills and are sometimes heard tinkling silver bells.

Lieschi ("Wood Spirit"): Russian fairies, who are always present in clumps of trees, particularly birch trees, and where the fly agaric mushroom grows.

Liminal: relating to a transitional or initial stage

Lugh: a king of the Tuatha Dé Danaan, a pan-Celtic god.

Lunatishee: Irish fairies that guard blackthorn trees.

Mab: a Welsh fairy queen.

Marzanna: the Polish personification of winter, a hag of death.

Meith: an Egyptian goddess, a magician titled "The Opener of the Ways" who conducted souls to the Otherworld, following a linen thread.

Menahune: Hawaiian house fairies.

Midsummer: the Midsummer Solstice, around 21st June. Because of calendar changes, Midsummer Day is now counted as 24th June.

Mittwinterfrau ("Lady of Midwinter"): a Croatian hag fairy who leads a procession of dead souls between Christmas and Twelfth Night. Her followers either reward or punish people, according to their desserts.

Moerae: A name for the ancient Greek Fates, the three goddesses who span, wove and cut the thread of destiny.

Morgan le Fay (Morgan the Fairy): the queen of the Isle of Avalon, who appears in Arthurian tales as his sister.

Moss Maidens: Female German forest spirits who protect the trees and spin the moss that hangs in the branches.

Munya: a Slavonic fairy who represents the lightning while her brothers are the two thunders.

Muse: a spirit of the Otherworld who brings inspiration to poets and artists.

Naecken: Swedish male water fairies who lure people to them by playing fiddles.

Nemetona: a Celtic grove used for sacred rituals and worship.

Norns: another name for the Wryd Sisters.

Numinous: having a strong religious or spiritual quality.

Nymphs: female nature spirits of Greek myth; different nymphs live in the sea, rivers, lakes, meadows, mountains and so on.

Oakmen: English fairies that live in the saplings that grow from felled oaks.

Oberon: The king of the fairies in Shakespeare's *A Midsummer Night's Dream.*

Oisin: the son of the Irish hero Finn Mac Cool, who journeyed to the Fairyland.

Otherworld: the realm of fairies and spirits that overlies our own world, usually unseen except in special circumstances.

Pans: a race of male nature fairies with goat attributes. They may have been the precursors of the god Pan.

Parcae: the Roman goddess of Fate.

Pegasos (Latin Pegasus): the winged horse of Apollo and the Muses in Greek myth.

Pelze Nicol: "Furry Nicholas," from his fur costume.

Perchta: a Germanic/Slavonic fairy who carries the souls of dead and yet-to-be-born children around with her as she tends the plants.

Persephone: in Greek myth the daughter of Demeter and goddess of spring, who has to spend part of the year in the underworld. She is associated with European fairy-lore.

Phooka: a malicious Irish fairy.

Pixies: fairies found only in the southwest of England who led travellers astray, but who helped kindly farmers with their work.

Polevik: fairies of the Russian cornfields that grow with the grain and after the harvest shrink to the size of the stubble.

Polewiki: fairies of the Polish cornfields that grow with the grain and after the harvest shrink to the size of the stubble

Prana: in Hinduism the breath, considered as a life-giving force.

Pripoldnica ("Midday Spirit"): who looks like a young woman carrying a sickle.

Puck: a mischievous English fairy.

Queen of Elphame: the Scottish term for the fairy queen.

Rân: the queen of mermaids and water fairies. She was originally a Norse goddess, the wife of Aegir, the sea god.

Rhiannon: A Welsh horse riding goddess, possibly cognate with Epona, whose seven blackbirds called dreamers into Fairyland.

Robin Goodfellow: a mischievous English fairy of the woodlands.

Runa: a charm or spell.

Rusalki: Russian water fairies or wood nymphs.

Salamanders: Elemental spirits of Fire.

Salvanelli: Italian fairies that raise storms to ride on the wind

Samhain: the Celtic festival that marked the start of winter on 1st November.

Samogorska: a Southern Slavonic mountain

fairy who inhabits the high peaks, hilltops or sometimes in the valleys.

Seefräuline: a German lake maiden.

Selkies: Scottish fairies who normally have the appearance of grey seals, but occasionally shed their skins to become human and dance upon the seashore.

Shaitans: originally Arabic spirits, a type of muse or genius inspiring poets and prophets.

Shvod: a house fairy of North American folklore. He is usually helpful, but parents sometimes refer to him as a kind of bogeyman as a threat to coerce children unto good behaviour.

Sidhe: the Celtic term for fairies, a word that means a burial mound, hill, or earth barrow.

Sileni: creatures of classical Greek myth, similar to satyrs. In appearance, they have horses' ears and sometimes the legs of horses or goats, too.

Sinend: daughter of Lodan son of Lir, often visited a well in Fairyland. There stood the hazels of wisdom and inspiration that in the same hour bore fruit, blossom, and foliage that fell upon the well in the same shower. On one occasion the waters broke forth in anger and overwhelmed her, washing her up on the shore of the river Shannon where she died giving the river its name.

Skosrå: Swedish wood spirits that are present whenever a violent whirlwind appears and the trees are shaken to breaking point.

Sluagh ("Fairy Host"): malevolent Highland fairies, the Hosts of the Unforgiven Dead, damned souls of dead humans forced to haunt the scene of their sins forever. They fly about in black clouds like starlings, up and down the face of the earth, haunting the scenes of their sins.

Spriggans ("Spirits"): Cornish fairies that keep treasure beneath the old stones.

St Elmo's Fire: a type of Will o'the Wisp that appears at sea (thought by scientists to be caused by electrical discharges during thunderstorms). It is accompanied by a crackling sound and is seen on ships' masts. When sailors see it they know that the worst of the storm is over and once asserted that the lights were the souls of the drowned.

Sumske Dekle ("Woodland Maidens"): Croatian woodland fairy maidens, covered in hair.

Sylvans: Greek woodland fairies, beautiful but dangerous. They lure travellers to their deaths in the forests.

Tennin: lovely fairy maidens of Buddhist lore, sometimes encountered on the highest summit of the mountains.

Tinkerbell: a fairy invented by J.M.Barrie in his play, *Peter Pan*.

Trows: misshapen fairies from Orkney.

Tuatha Dé Danaan: pre-Celtic inhabitants of Ireland who were a race of gods, who following the Celtic invasion, retreated from the world into the mounds, and became fairies.

Tugen: the feathered cloak worn by Celtic bards

Twyleth Teg: the Welsh fairy folk.

Unseelie Court ("Unblessed Court"): unpleasant Scottish fairies.

Vadleany ("Forest Girl"): a forest fairy of Hungarian lore, who appears as a naked girl with hair so long that it sweeps the ground.

Vesna: fairies that live in Slovenian mountain palaces and influence the fates of both men and crops.

Vile ("Whirlwind"): Slavonic fairies that dwell in woodlands; some of the forest Vily are connected with particular trees in the manner of dryads and cannot venture far from them.

Vilenice: a witch in Slavonic culture who learns her craft from the fairies.

Vivienne or **Nimue:** a lady of the lake who appears in the stories of King Arthur, supplying him with Excalibur, a magical fairy sword.

Walker between the Worlds: a person, perhaps a shaman or witch, who travels to the Otherworld and back again at will.

Washer at the Ford: a Scottish fairy who appears washing clothes in a stream and who is an omen of death.

Wassail: a toast, especially one made to the spirits of the apple trees in Britain.

White Lady: a generic name for female fairies in many parts of the world, particularly those who are guardians of particular places, such as mountain passes, fountains, wells, and fords.

Wiccan: an Anglo-Saxon term for a witch who deals with the spirits of the natural world.

Wicce (wise one): Anglo-Saxon term for a witch, male or female.

Wild Hunt: a collection of spirits that rides out, under the leadership of the likes of Herne, King Arthur, or Wod, to collect the souls of the dead.

Wild Men: shaggy forest spirits known in Britain and continental Europe.

Will o' the Wisp: a fairy that appears as a small light darting around bogs and marshy places.

Wise Woman: a term for the female village witch or shaman in Britain.

Wod: a Wild Huntsman who, mounted on a white horse and accompanied by his pack of ferocious hounds, accosts lonely travellers.

Wood-wives: German forest fairies.

Woodwose: another name for a wild man, they have a shaggy appearance, often naked and covered only in their own hair.

Wotan or **Woden:** the shamanic god of the Germanic peoples who journeyed into the Otherworld to gain visions and the secret of the runes.

Wyrd Sisters: in Anglo-Saxon myth, the three fates who guard the cosmic axis or world tree.

Yule: the Anglo-Saxon term for the Winter Solstice, or shortest day, around 21st December.

Zephyrs: fairy guardians of the winds in Greek lore.

Select
Bibliography

Anderson, Hans Christian. *Fairy Tales. city, state/country*:
Edmund Ward, 1958.

Arrowsmith, Nancy. *A Field Guide to the Little People.*
London: Macmillan, 1977.

Bloom, William. *Working with Angels, Fairies and
Nature Spirits.* London: Piatkus Ltd., 1998.

Branston, Brian. *The Lost Gods of England.* London:
Thames and Hudson, 1957.

Carmichael, Alexander. *Carmina Gadelica.*Edinburgh:
Oliver and Boyd, 1928.

Croker, T. Crofton. *Fairy Legends and Traditions of
the South of Ireland.* London: John Murray, 1826.

Franklin, Anna. *Illustrated Encyclopaedia of Fairies.*
London: Paper Tiger, 2004.

————.*Fairy Lore*. Chieveley, England: Capall
Bann, 2000.

————.*The Fairy Ring*. St. Paul, Minn.: Llewellyn,
2002.

Geoffrey of Monmouth, *Vita Merlini.* Cardoff, England: University of Wales Press, 1973.

Giraldus Cambrensis. *The Historical Works.* Ed. Thomas Wright. London: Bohn, 1863.

Grimm, Wilhelm and Jacob. *The German Legends* (trans. Donald Ward). Philadelphia: Institute for the Study of Human Issues, 1981.

Guest, Charlotte, and J. Jones (trans.). *Mabinogion.* Wales, England.: University of Wales Press, 1977.

Keightley, Thomas. *The Fairy Mythology.* London: Whittaker, Treacher and Co., 1833

Kirk, Robert. *The Secret Commonwealth of Elves, Fauns and Fairies* (1691). London: The Folk-lore Society, 1976.

MacManus, D.A. *The Middle Kingdom.* Colin Smythe Ltd., Gerrards Croos, Bucks: 1979.

Miller, Hugh. *The Old Red Sandstone.* Edinburgh, 1841.

Moore, A.W. *Manx Folk-lore.* Douglas, 1899.

Morrison, Sophia. *Manx Fairy Tales,* Nutt, London, 1911.

Murray, Margaret. *Witch Cult in Western Europe.* Oxford: Oxford University Press, 1921.

Palmer, Roy. *The Folk-lore of Warwickshire.* London: Batsford, 1976.

Sikes, Wirt. *British Goblins: The Realm of the Faerie.* 1880.

Spence, Lewis. *The Fairy Tradition in Britain.* London: Rider, 1948.

Tongue, R.L. *Somerset Folk-lore: County Series VIII.* London: Folk Lore Society, 1965.

Wentz, Evans, *The Fairy Faith in Celtic Countries.* Franklin Lakes, N.J.: New Page Books, 2004.

Wilde, Lady. *Ancient Legends, Mystic Charms and Superstitions off Ireland.* London: Ward and Downey, 1878.

Yeats, W.B. *Folk and Fairy Tales of the Irish Peasantry,* London: Walter Scott, 1888.

Index

241

N

O

About the Author

Anna Franklin was born in Derbyshire, in England, and grew up in a small town in Leicestershire, in the English Midlands. She was educated at a Roman Catholic convent school, followed by a grammar school, then spent a gap year working on a local newspaper. After doing some travelling in Europe, Anna went to art college, completing a foundation course at Nuneaton Art School and subsequently an honours degree in fine art at the Lanchester Polytechnic, specializing in photography. During the next few years Anna worked as a press photographer, as a seaside photographer, for a sports photographer, and as a community artist. She had many exhibitions during this period and won Cosmopolitan Young Photographer of the Year. She also taught photography, video, watercolour painting, and drawing.

Initiated into the Craft at the age of 18, Anna studied with an Alexandrian/Gardnerian coven, then later Traditional Wicce with Sara and Phil Robinson of the Coranieid, from whom she received her second degree. In the mid 1980s Anna founded the Hearth of Arianrhod, running teaching circles, outer circles, and working coven and postal courses, along with publishing the Pagan magazine *Silver Wheel*. Anna's third degree came from Merrymoon, the coven's Gardnerian high priest. At this time, Anna began to concentrate on her Craft activities, and was soon a familiar sight at psychic fairs and magical gatherings with the *Silver Wheel* stall, and began to supply many of Britain's occult shops with ritually prepared incenses and magickal oils, aromatherapy, and perfume oils. Having already studied Craft herbalism, Anna now gained qualifications as a reflexologist and aromatherapist and founded the Holistic Healing Centre.

She has contributed hundreds of articles to both small press and professional magazines, and has written more than 20 books including *Herb Craft*, *Familiars*, *Pagan Feasts*, *Personal Power*, *The Wellspring*, *Fairy Lore*, *Magical Incenses and Oils*, *The Sacred Circle Tarot*, *The Fairy Ring*, *The Illustrated Encyclopaedia of Fairies*, *Midsummer*, and *Lammas*. Many of these books have been illustrated by Paul Mason, a friend since her art college days.

Anna still runs the Hearth of Arianrhod, which includes a working coven, outer circle, day courses, correspondence course, a magazine called *Silver Wheel*, and a newsletter.

Anna lives in a village in the English Midlands with her partner John, six cats, and numerous chickens. Between them they grow most of their own fruit, vegetables, and herbs and try to live the Pagan life while simultaneously conducting a love affair with Egypt and dreaming of owning a winter home in Luxor!